TABLE OF CONTENTS

FOREWORD. 4

MEET OUR PUPPETS 5

All Year 'Round. 6
The Very Worried Worm 8
Al the Gator. 10
The Joy Secret 12
Elroy's Diet 14
Horoscope Horror. 16
Noah's Ark. 18
Lost and Found 20
Feeding the Five Thousand. 22
The Good Samaritan 24
Did You Hear Me Cry?. 26
Come to VBS 28
Discovery. 29
I'm So Angry. 30
"I" Trouble. 32
I Love My Sunday School. 35
A Christmas Poem. 36
I Am Thankful. 39
Why In the World?. 41

SONGS FOR PUPPETS TO SING

All Year 'Round 43
The Very Worried Worm 47
Al the Gator. 53
J-E-S-U-S 57
Noah's Ark. 59
Feeding the Five Thousand. 62
The Good Samaritan 66
Did You Hear Me Cry?. 68
Come to VBS 73
Discovery. 77
I'm So Angry. 80
Jesus and Me 87
I Love My Sunday School. 92
I Am Thankful. 95
See His Glory 99

HOW TO MAKE PUPPETS AND PUPPET STAGES 103

FOREWORD

Other than our faces, hands are the most expressive part of the human anatomy. An outstretched hand signifies openness and affection. A clenched fist represents anger or power. A firm handshake indicates friendship. A waving hand says good-bye. A held hand says, "I love you."

Though God is a Spirit, the Scriptures have much to say about His hands. His hands formed the universe (Psalm 19:1), strengthened His people (Psalm 18:35), brought judgment upon His enemies (1 Samuel 5:11), and reached out to man in love (Psalm 138:7; 139:5, 10). God's hands are the skillful hands of a creator (Psalm 139:13) and are like the hands of a potter (Jeremiah 18:6). Though toughened by the carpenter's trade, Jesus' hands felt the piercing pain of Calvary. The nail-prints in His hands were evidence of His resurrection (John 20:27). And now Jesus lives in glory at the right hand of God (Colossians 3:1).

God gave us hands. We can use them wisely or foolishly, lazily or busily, destructively or constructively. We can use our hands to write, to play, to work, to create. Even the ability to construct and manipulate a puppet is a God-given skill.

May all who hold this book in their hands use its pages to teach the truth of God. May the creations of our hands honor Him.

MEET OUR PUPPETS

Harold   A friendly little boy with a low, slow kind of voice; kindhearted, but not terribly perceptive; sometimes mischievous; often intimidated by Stella's domineering ways.

Stella   A rather egotistical little girl with a high, shrill voice; she can be strong-willed and impatient, but occasionally she lets her good side show.

Barney   A typical "kid next door"; a neutral personality with a rather ordinary voice.

Bernadette   A shy little girl whose shyness is matched by her sweetness; she speaks with a soft, slow, Southern drawl.

Grandpa Gray   A wise old gentleman who is loved and respected by all; he speaks with a mature, but sometimes feeble voice.

Grandma Gray   A sweet, matronly woman who, like her husband, speaks with a mature, but rather shaky voice.

Hobart the Worm   A long, green, lovable worm who is liked by others, but has a tendency to feel sorry for himself.

Elroy Elephant the Third   A big, blue elephant who is boastful and proud; he speaks with a sophisticated voice.

Clyde the Dog   A lovable brown dog with long, floppy ears and big, sad eyes.

Al the Gator   A big-eyed, fierce-looking but softhearted alligator who speaks with a sleepy, lazy voice and yawns frequently.

Kenny Cool   A confident, street-wise boy who wears sunglasses and the latest clothes; he is a smooth-talking leader who peppers his conversation with slang of the 1950s.

Note: You may want to use our characters, or you may want to change the names, or use your own characters. The plays are easily adaptable to your needs.

ALL YEAR 'ROUND

Characters: Harold
Stella

Harold (*enters, speaking thoughtfully*): Hmm. Let's see. There are twelve months in a year. There are thirty days in September, April, June, and November. All the rest have thirty-one, *except* for . . . *except* for—

Stella (*entering suddenly*): FEBRUARY! FEBRUARY! FEBRUARY!

Harold (*startled*): Uh, I *beg* your pardon?

Stella: I said, "February," Harold! The month of February has only twenty-eight days, except in a leap year, and then it has twenty-nine days.

Harold: Oh, yeah—February. Boy, Stella, how do you know so much about the calendar?

Stella: Well, Harold, when a girl is as busy as I am, she has to follow the calendar closely. I'm busy, busy, busy!

Harold: Yeah, being a nag must take lots of time.

Stella: Harold, I *am not a nag!* I just happen to be a perfectionist where others are concerned.

Harold: Well, whoop-dee-do for you too!

Stella: Let's get back to the point, Harold. I have a very busy schedule. I have an appointment on Tuesday to play with Bernadette and on Thursday I'm going shopping with Grandma Gray and on Friday I'm having my hair done . . . .

Harold: Well done, I hope. Right now it looks medium rare!

Stella: Well, Harold, at least *I* know the months of the year. I bet you don't even know what the four seasons are.

Harold: The four seasons? Sure I do.

Stella: OK, then. What *are* the four seasons, Harold?

Harold: The four seasons . . . OK . . . well, there's . . . uh . . . pepper, and salt, and oregano if you're Italian, and chili powder if you're Mexican! Yep, that makes four!

Stella: Oh, Harold, those aren't *seasons.* Those are *seasonings.*

Harold (*embarrassed*): Oh, yeah.

Stella: The four seasons are winter, spring, summer, and autumn. Which one is your favorite, Harold?

Harold: I like autumn, 'cause I like to play football.

Stella: I like winter, because I like playing in the snow and sitting around a warm fire.

Harold: I like spring, 'cause everything turns warm and green.

Stella: And I like summer, because that's

when my parents take me to the beach.

Harold *(thoughtfully)*: You know something, Stella?

Stella: What's that, Harold?

Harold: We might have favorite seasons of the year, and the weather and the trees and the months might change; but there's one thing that never changes.

Stella: What's that, Harold?

Harold: *God* never changes. Just knowing that He's around all the time gives me joy, no matter what time of year it is.

Stella: You know, you're right for once, Harold. Even on those cold wintry days, knowing I'm part of God's family makes me feel like a winner.

Harold: And in the spring, when new life is popping up all around, I just feel like singing praises to God.

Stella *(getting excited)*: And in the summer, when it's hot and things are growing fast and strong, I need to grow too—becoming more like God wants me to be!

Harold: And when the cool weather comes , it makes me feel invinegarated!

Stella: That's *invigorated,* Harold.

Harold: Oh, well, you get the idea.

(Harold and Stella sing "All Year Round," music on page 43.)

Verse 1:

He: In the winter I'm a winner.
She: In the springtime I can sing la-la-la!
He: In the summer I'm a becomer,
Both: And in the autumn up and at 'em with a zing!

Chorus:

Both: All year 'round, we bring all our days to the Lord.
All year 'round, we sing and give praise to the Lord.

Verse 2:

She: In the winter I'm a winner;
He: In the springtime robins call.
She: In the summer I remember,
He: That in the autumn I'll never fall.
(Speaking): Ha, ha—get it? "In the *autumn* I'll never *fall!* Ha, ha, ha!)

(Repeat chorus and first verse.)

THE VERY WORRIED WORM

Characters: Hobart the Worm
Grandpa Gray

(Grandpa and Hobart enter.)

Grandpa: Well, hello, Hobart. How are you today?

Hobart: Oh, I'm worried, Grandpa Gray.

Grandpa: Worried?

(Hobart sings "The Very Worried Worm," words and music on page 47.)

Chorus, verse 1:
Chorus, verse 2:

Grandpa: Uh, Hobart?

Hobart: Yes, Grandpa Gray?

Grandpa: Let me ask you a question. What would you advise me to do if I had a bad habit?

Hobart: A bad habit? Like what, Grandpa Gray?

Grandpa: Well, for example . . . what if I ate five hundred donuts every day? That would be a bad habit, don't you think?

Hobart: Grandpa Gray, if you ate five hundred donuts every day, you'd weigh five hundred pounds!

Grandpa: And what advice would you give me, Hobart?

Hobart: I'd tell you that you needed to change that bad habit or it would hurt you.

Grandpa: And how could I change?

Hobart: Well, you'd have to decide to change your eating habits, that's for sure! You'd need to eat some other foods that are good for you, like grains and vegetables and fruit.

Grandpa: That's right! Now, Hobart, since you're my friend, I want to help you with a bad habit you seem to have.

Hobart (*hesitantly*): You mean . . . you've noticed?

Grandpa (*compassionately*): Yes, I have, Hobart.

Hobart (*hanging his head in shame*): Oh, I'm so ashamed, Grandpa Gray. I promise I'll never sneak cookies from the cookie jar again!

Grandpa (*surprised*): No, no, no, Hobart. I'm not talking about sneaking cookies from the cookie jar!

Hobart: Then what bad habit do you *mean*, Grandpa Gray?

Grandpa: I'm talking about your habit of *worrying!* Eating five hundred donuts every day would hurt a person, that's for sure. But Hobart, *worrying* every day can hurt a person too!

Hobart: But, Grandpa, I worry about things because . . . well, because I'm *concerned* about what might happen.

Grandpa: Concern is good, Hobart. But just like donuts, *too* much of a good thing can

be destructive! Worrying doesn't help you find answers to problems.

Hobart: You know, I've noticed that, Grandpa Gray. Worrying doesn't seem to change anything for the better.

Grandpa: That right! And besides, many times we worry about things that really aren't problems at all!

Hobart: But how can I learn to *quit* worrying, Grandpa?

Grandpa: Well, you said if I wanted to quit eating all those donuts, I'd have to *decide* to change. That's the place to begin in overcoming worry, Hobart.

Hobart: And then, I said you'd need to substitute healthier foods for some of those donuts.

Grandpa: That's right! And, you see, Hobart, you need to substitute healthier thoughts and healthier actions for some of those worries you have.

Hobart: OK, Grandpa, that makes sense.

Grandpa: And, Hobart, it helps to remember what the Bible says. First Peter 5:7 says to give all your worries to God, because He cares for you. And in Matthew chapter six, Jesus says we shouldn't worry about what we will eat or drink or wear. God will take care of you, Hobart! Learn to trust Him more—*that's* the best solution to worry!

Hobart: But, Grandpa Gray, there's still one thing that bothers me.

Grandpa: What's that?

Hobart: You don't *really* eat five hundred donuts a day, do you, Grandpa?

Grandpa (*laughs*): No, I'd say four hundred fifty is my limit!

Hobart (*cheerfully*): Oh, Grandpa Gray, you've helped me to be happy again!

(*Sings reprise of "The Very Worried Worm."*)

I will learn to be content, and worries I'll do
    without;
Worries I'll do without, worries I'll do with-
    out.
For as long as God is with me, surely I
    shouldn't doubt;
Worries I'll do without, what should I worry
    about?

And so if I trust the Lord to see me through
    each passing day;
And if I fill my time with wholesome work
    and wholesome play;
And if I learn to serve the Lord in what I do
    and say,
These healthy things will crowd the worry
    out!

Hobart and **Grandpa** (*Sing together*):

We will learn to be content, and worries we'
    do without;
Worries we'll do without, worries we'll do
    without.
For as long as God is with us, surely
    shouldn't doubt;
Worries we'll do without, what should we
    worry about?
For as long as God is with us, surely
    shouldn't doubt.

Hobart (*sings alone*): I'm a worry-free, a
wonderf'ly—wiser worm!

AL THE GATOR

Characters: Al the Gator
           Hobart the Worm

(The play begins with Al the Gator snoring loudly. Hobart the Worm enters, but doesn't notice Al the Gator.)

Hobart: Oh, this *sure is* a nice day. *(Sees Al the Gator, acts surprised and frightened.)* Oh, dear! HELP! An alligator! Oh, my! I'm so scared of alligators! HELP!

Al *(waking up)*: What's all that shouting about? What's going on? Can't a guy get a decent nap around here?

Hobart *(nervously)*: Oh, excuse me, Mister Alligator, Sir. Uh . . . you see . . . I was just taking a little walk. I didn't mean to disturb you. As a matter of fact, I was just leaving! 'Bye! *(Starts to leave.)*

Al: Wait a minute there, little fellow. We haven't even been introduced yet. Let me tell you about myself.

(Al sings, "Al the Gator," music on page 53, while Hobart acts nervous.)

I'm a 'gator, "Al the Gator."
And I'd rather meetcha now than later.
'Cause later on I'll be
Napping 'neath a tree,
And I don't need a pesky aggravator!

I'm a 'gator, "Al the Gator."
And I love to sleep, there's nothing
    greater.
But I'll wake up, you see,
When someone brings to me

A scrumptious meal served by a fancy
    waiter!
I'm a 'gator, "Al the Gator."
And I'd rather meetcha now than later.
I'm a lazy guy, you see
I'd be crazy not to be,
'Cause a lazy life's the only life for me!
(Yawns widely.)

Hobart: Well, it's nice to meet you, Mr. Gator. *(Nervously starts to leave again.)* Like I said, I was just leaving.

Al: Oh, worm, it takes too much effort to call me "Mr. Gator." You can just call me Al. Hey, what did you say your name is?

Hobart *(still frightened)*: My n-n-name is Hobart, Sir . . . I mean, my name is Hobart, Mr. Gator . . . I mean, my name is Hobart, Al.

Al: Well, Hobart, why are you so nervous?

Hobart: Well . . . ah . . . you're an . . . an— ALLIGATOR! Aren't you going to try to eat me?

Al: Me? Eat you? Nah. I'm too lazy to bother.

Hobart: Too lazy?

Al: Yeah, I just sleep all day long. I love to sleep. That's my hobby.

Hobart: Don't you ever *(gulp)* eat?

Al: Oh, when the mood strikes. *(Hobart backs away.)* But mostly I just sleep. So

10

why don't you scram now, so I can get some rest?

Hobart: Well, OK. *(Hesitates, becomes more confident.)* But wait a minute, Mr. Alligator, I mean, Al. What kind of life is that? I mean, if all you do is sleep all the time, how do you ever find time to enjoy life?

Al: I *am* enjoying life! I *like* being lazy. Now run along, Hobart. I'm trying to take my nap, you know!

Hobart: Excuse me for saying so, Al, but I don't think a lazy life is a very smart way to live.

Al: Who *cares?*

Hobart: Well, *God* cares! He put you on this beautiful earth for a reason. You have a job to do. You shouldn't waste your life by being lazy.

Al: Who cares?

Hobart: Your *friends* care!

Al: What friends? I don't have any friends. I'm too lazy to make any friends.

Hobart: You don't have any friends? Why, that's terrible. You're missing out on a lot of fun!

Al: Boy, Hobart. I've never thought about the things you're saying. Am I really missing out on all the good things in life?

Hobart: You sure are. God wants you to use your time wisely. He wants you to be creative and healthy and have good friendly relationships. God doesn't want you to overwork, but He never meant for you to sleep your life away, either!

Al: As much as I hate to admit it, I think you're right. It's not good to be lazy. Will you help me to be a better alligator?

Hobart: Sure. I'd love to be your friend and help you, Al.

(Al sings reprise of "Al the Gator.")
I'm a 'gator, "Al the Gator."
Guess I had to learn it sooner or later;
That laziness, you see,
is not so good for me.

(Hobart sings):
As a friend indeed, I'm not a hesitator!
You're a 'gator, "Al the Gator."
And I've never known a 'gator who was greater.

(Al sings):
From now on you will see,
I'll be busy as a bee.
'Cause the busy life's the only life for me!
Yes, a busy life's the only life for me!

Hobart: Well, Al, I'm glad I was able to help. I have to be going now. See ya later, Alligator! *(He leaves.)*

Al: Oh, boy, all that singing made me thirsty! I think I'll go get some gator-aid! *(He leaves.)*

THE JOY SECRET

Characters: Grandma Gray
Harold

Grandma *(enters, humming cheerfully)*: Oh, my! What a lovely day! The sun is shining, the birds are chirping. I feel so happy today! *(She continues humming.)*

Harold *(entering)*: Hi, Grandma Gray. Do you mind if I visit for a while?

Grandma *(pleasantly)*: Why, even though my name is Grandma *Gray, I'm* just tickled *pink* to see you, Harold! I just finished making some pink lemonade. Would you like some, Harold?

Harold *(thoughtfully)*: No, thanks, Grandma. I'm glad you're tickled pink. But actually, *I've* been feeling a little *blue!*

Grandma: Really? Is there something you want to talk to me about?

Harold: Well, I've been wondering . . . *(hesitates.)* Oh, never mind.

Grandma: Now, Harold, don't be shy. You can talk to me about *anything*—anything at all.

Harold: Oh, Grandma, I know you're old and wise . . . *(stammers a bit.)* I . . . I mean, you're wise and old . . . I mean . . . you're not just old, you're also pretty smart . . . I mean—

Grandma *(laughing kindly)*: Now, Harold, you can relax. I know I'm a few years older than you are. But I can still be your friend.

Harold: Thanks, Grandma. It's just that . . . well, I don't think you would understand.

Grandma: Really?

Harold: Well, you always seem so cheerful and happy. It seems like nothing ever gets you down.

Grandma *(nodding)*: Yes, I must say I feel rather cheerful today. Why, who wouldn't feel happy on such a beautiful day as this?

Harold: Actually, Grandma, I don't feel very cheerful at all today. None of my friends are around to play with me. My mom is in a grouchy mood. There's nothing good to eat in the refrigerator. And I just feel kind of sad inside.

Grandma: Well, Harold, everyone has bad days once in a while. *(Chuckles.)* Jesus promised us "everlasting life," but I don't think he ever promised we'd have an "ever-laughing life"!

Harold: But nothing ever seems to bother you, Grandma.

Grandma: Oh, Harold, everyone has troubles in life. I've had my share of problems.

Harold *(surprised)*: Even you, Grandma? What kind of problems do *old* people have? *(Stammers again)* I . . . I mean . . . I'm not saying that just because you're old, you're over the hill . . . I mean—

Grandma *(laughing)*: Oh Harold, we older folks have our aches and pains, and some-

12

times we feel some regrets and sadness. As my husband, Grandpa Gray, says, "Sometime life hurts—and there's no ouchless answer!"

Harold: But Grandma, you always seem so full of joy!

Grandma *(softly)*: Harold, let me tell you a little secret.

Harold: A secret? I love secrets!

Grandma: In fact, I call this my *joy secret*, Harold. *(Whispers something in Harold's ear.)*

Harold *(out loud)*: J-E-S-U-S? That's your secret? J-E-S-U-S spells "Jesus"!

Grandma *(nodding)*: Yes, Harold. That's my joy secret. Jesus is my special friend. The Bible says Jesus himself went through a lot of suffering. He understands my hurts, and He helps me through the rough times.

Harold: But *how*, Grandma? What about the times when you feel weak and all alone?

Grandma: Those are the times I rely on my special verses!

Harold: Your special verses? Is this another one of your secrets, Grandma?

Grandma *(laughing)*: Oh, Harold. There's nothing secret about it! My special verses are right there in the Bible for anyone to read. They give me special comfort and strength when I feel down.

Harold: So what are these special verses, Grandma?

Grandma: Well, here are some of my favorites: "Give all your worries to him, because he cares for you." That's found in 1 Peter 5:7. "The joy of the Lord will make you strong," is found in Nehemiah 8:10. "My help comes from the Lord. He made heaven and earth" is from Psalm 121:2.

Harold: Hmm . . . J-E-S-U-S! I'm going to remember your joy secret.

Grandma: That's right, Harold. Even when hard times come, I just rely on Jesus and His promises. He never lets me down!

(She sings "J-E-S-U-S," music on page 57.)

Chorus:
    J - E - S - U - S
    Jesus is the very best.
    He brought peace, joy, a love that's
        true—
    Jesus can be your friend too.

(Repeat chorus.)

    Got a song in my heart
        And a smile on my face;
    Feelin' happy, kinda scrappy,
        Any time, any place.
    Got a peace in my heart
        That I just can't erase—
    And it's all because of His wonderful
        grace!

(Repeat chorus.)

Harold: Thanks for the encouragement, Grandma Gray!

Grandma: Now are you ready for some of that pink lemonade, Harold?

Harold: Sure! And you know what? I think I'll come back and talk to you again tomorrow!

ELROY'S DIET

Characters:
    Elroy Elephant the Third
    Hobart the Worm
    Stella

(Hobart and Elroy enter.)

Elroy: Oh, hi, Hobart. What have you been doing lately?

Hobart: Funny you should ask, Elroy. I've been reading a book that might interest you.

Elroy: What kind of book? Is it a book about my favorite subject?

Hobart: No, it's not a book about peanuts, Elroy.

Elroy: Oh, no, I hope it's not a book about my *least* favorite subject.

Hobart: No, it's not a book about mice, Elroy!

Elroy *(relieved)*: Boy, am I glad!

Hobart: No, Elroy, this is a book about *self-improvement.*

Elroy: Self-improvement? Why should I read a book about self-improvement, Hobart? You know as well as I do that my personality is absolutely *impeccable!*

Hobart: Well, your *personality* may be impeccable. But if you ask me, there are plenty of other things about you that are *very* "peccable."

Elroy *(surprised)*: Oh?

Hobart: Yes, Elroy. *(Nods.) It's* not your personality, but, well—

Elroy: C'mon, Hobart. I can take it. Tell me, what about me needs to be changed?

Hobart *(timidly)*: It's your *weight,* Elroy.

Elroy: My *what?*

Hobart: Not your what; your weight.

Elroy *(indignantly)*: And what is wrong with my weight?

Hobart: Well, you do weigh five tons, don't you?

Elroy: Well, yes—

Hobart: And you'd feel better about yourself if you lost a few hundred pounds, right?

Elroy: Well, now that you mention it.—

Hobart: And you haven't been able to stick to a diet, have you?

Elroy *(shaking head sadly)*: No.

Hobart: And why *haven't* you stuck to your diet?

Elroy: Well, for one thing, those Weight Watcher peanuts tasted awful! And whenever I tried to eat lettuce, it clogged up my trunk!

Hobart: Did you try cottage cheese?

Elroy: Yeah, but the owner of the cottage told me to get lost.

Hobart: Oh, Elroy, I think you should just try a simple medical technique I learned in this self-improvement book. Here's what you do. First, get comfortable.

Elroy *(nodding)*: OK.

Hobart: Are you comfortable?

Elroy: Yes.

Hobart: Well, I'm not! You're standing on the end of me! Ouch!

Elroy *(jumping off)*: Oh, I beg your pardon!

Hobart: C'mon, Elroy, just relax.

Stella *(entering)*: Hey, what are you guys doing?

Hobart: I'm teaching Elroy some self-improvement techniques.

Elroy: Yeah, and you know what, Stella?

Stella: What, Elroy?

Elroy: Hobart's idea here seems to be working. In fact, I'm sure it's working. I'm not hungry!

Stella *(matter-of-factly)*: The reason you're not hungry, Elroy, is that you just finished your lunch ten minutes ago.

Elroy: I did?

Stella: Yes—fifty pounds of peanuts! I couldn't believe it. *Fifty pounds!*

Elroy: It was just a little snack—

Hobart: And my advice might be helping— the book was written by a *true* expert on human nature.

Stella: Maybe so, Hobart. But I know a Book whose Author is *truly* an expert on human nature. This Book is *unbeatable* for improving people.

Elroy and **Hobart:** Oh yeah? What book is that?

Stella: It's the *Bible.* The Bible gives us good, practical guidelines for living. And it tells us that, through prayer, God will give us strength to change the things we can and accept the things we *can't* change.

Elroy: You mean God can even help me deal with my weight problem?

Stella: Sure, Elroy. And in the meantime, we love you just the way you are, big guy.

(Hobart and Stella move closer and lean their heads against Elroy.)

Elroy *(bashfully)*: Oh, *you guys!*

(All leave.)

HOROSCOPE HORROR

Characters: Grandma Gray
Grandpa Gray

Grandma: Let's see, now. My birthday is June 17. That means I'm a Gemini. And the number to call is . . . let's see, now . . . where did I put that telephone number?

Grandpa (*entering*): What are you looking for, Grandma?

Grandma: Just a telephone number, Grandpa. I wrote it down on a piece of paper and now I can't seem to remember where I put it. I guess I'm getting old and forgetful.

Grandpa: Here, let me help you find it. (*Moves closer to her.*) What was the telephone number *for*, anyway?

Grandma: Oh, it's a new service called "Horoscopes by Phone."

Grandpa (*shocked*): You mean you are going to make a telephone call to get your horoscope reading for the day?

Grandma (*nodding*): That's right, Grandpa.

Grandpa: But Grandma, I'm surprised at you! You don't believe in that stuff, do you?

Grandma: Well, I'm not sure, Grandpa. Yesterday, Henrietta called and said her horoscope told her to "devise new ways to save money." Then last night at the women's meeting, our subject for discussion just happened to be "How to Save Money by Coupon Shopping." I just thought—

Grandpa (*interrupting*): Now, just a minute, Grandma. (*His* voice *becomes impatient.*) Just a minute! Do you know where these horoscopes come from?

Grandma: Well, they're based on the stars, I suppose. The predictions have to do with the position of the stars when you were born.

Grandpa (*nodding*): That's right. And why do people read horoscopes?

Grandma: There are lots of reasons. I guess they want to know how to plan their lives and get the most out of life.

Grandpa: Well, Grandma, do you think we get the best advice from the stars or from Jesus Christ?

Grandma: Why, from Jesus, of course.

Grandpa: And, Grandma, do you know what the Bible says about following the stars?

Grandma: Well, I know the wise men followed the star at Jesus' birth.

Grandpa: True, true. But that was a special act of God. You can't find any Scriptures that tell us to plan our lives according to the stars *or* our birth dates.

Grandma: Oh, dear.

Grandpa: And, Grandma, the prophet Isaiah warned us that astrology can't do us any good in the end—it can't change our lives or save us. *(Isaiah 47:13-15.)*

Grandma: Oh, Grandpa, I didn't realize that!

Grandpa: It's true. *(Nods vigorously.)*

Grandma: Then, I guess God doesn't want His children getting involved in things like that.

Grandpa: Right! Anything that gets in the way of our trusting God and worshiping Him becomes like a god to us. So God warns us to stay away from it. In fact, Grandma, if we start living by our horoscopes, we might easily forget to put Christ first and let *Him* direct our lives.

Grandma *(looking around from side to side)*: Oh, where did I put that telephone number?

Grandpa *(annoyed)*: Grandma, you're not going to call now, are you? I thought you understood what I was saying about horoscopes.

Grandma: I did understand, Grandpa. I don't want the phone number for "Horoscopes by Phone." I want *Henrietta's* number. I want to call *her* and tell *her* what you just told me. *(She snuggles up against him.)* You sure are a wise man, Grandpa.

Grandpa *(embarrassed)*: Aw, shucks, Grandma.

(They leave together.)

NOAH'S ARK

Characters:
> **Elroy Elephant the Third**
> **Hobart the Worm**
> **Clyde the Dog**
> **Al the Gator**

Elroy: Hobart! Come quickly! It's time for the Bible story where we are the stars!

Hobart *(entering)*: Hi, Elroy. What's going on? What are you so excited about?

Elroy: Hobart, didn't you hear what I said? I said, it's time for the Bible story where we are the stars!

Hobart: Stars? You and me?

Elroy *(nodding vigorously)*: Yes, you and me, and Clyde the Dog and Al the Gator.

(Clyde and Al enter.)

Al *(lazily)*: Did someone mention my name?

Clyde: Woof! Woof!

Elroy: Yes, indeed! Now that we're all here, let's get on with it.

Al *(lazily)*: On with *what?* What's going on around here?

Hobart: Oh, Elroy says that it's time to do a Bible story where we are the stars!

Clyde: Stars? Woof, woof!

Elroy: Yes, that's right. Now can anyone guess which Bible story I'm thinking about?

Clyde: Not me! Nope! Not me! Woof, woof!

Al: Why don't you just tell us, Elroy? I'm too lazy to play a guessing game.

Hobart: That's all right, Elroy. Al is too lazy to play *any* kind of game! Go ahead and give us a clue, Elroy.

Elroy: Well, this particular story involves *animals. Lots* of animals. That, by the way, is why we are the stars of the story.

Hobart: A story about animals. Well, I can think of *lots* of Bible stories with animals. Give us another clue, Elroy.

Elroy: Well, this story involves *water. Lots* of water.

Al: I like the water, but I still don't know which story you're talking about. How about another clue?

Clyde: Bark! Bark!

Elroy: You're getting close! This story is about something that rhymes with "bark."

Hobart *(thoughtfully)*: Hmm . . . a story with lots of animals, lots of water, and something that rhymes with "bark." What could it be? *(To the audience)*: Kids, can you help us out? *(Children call out, "Noah's ark.")*

Elroy: That's it—Noah's ark! My, my, what a smart bunch we have out there. Since you kids are so smart, maybe you could help us tell the story. OK? Well, it all started when God told a man that there was going to be a flood! You see, the whole earth was full of sin—except for this one man and his family. What was that man's name, kids? *(Children call out, "Noah.")*

Elroy: Very good, very good! Then God told Noah that he and his family would be saved from a big flood that was coming on the earth. God instructed Noah to build a big boat. What was that boat called, kids? *(Children call out, "Ark.")*

Elroy: Right again. Excellent! My, you kids really know your Bible story.

Al: Oh, I know what happened next. God told Noah to put all kinds of animals on the ark. Like alligators.

Clyde: And dogs. Woof!

Hobart: And worms, too.

Elroy: And of course, let's not forget about the *elephants!* Yes, God saved Noah and his family and all the animals from the big flood that destroyed the earth.

Hobart: That's a nice story. God really blessed Noah because Noah was faithful. That's a good lesson for us all. Noah obeyed God, no matter what.

Al: Yep. We should always obey God, no matter what. We should obey God, just as Noah did.

Hobart: It's fun being the star of a story.

Elroy: It sure is! And now, for the grand finale, we are going to sing a special song for our wonderful audience. Here goes, a one and a two and a—

(All sing "Noah's Ark," music on page 59.)

Elroy: Elephants and worms and dogs—

Al: Alligators too.

Hobart:
We were all upon the ark.
Now we'll tell that story to you.

Elroy:
Well, God said, "Noah, better build a
  boat.

If you don't, you're never gonna stay
  afloat."
Noah listened to God and his family was
  saved.

Al: Oh yeah!

Clyde: Oh yeah!

Elroy: Walruses and porcupines and—

Al: Hopping kangaroos.

Hobart:
Things that crawl and climb and run—
It was really quite a zoo!

Elroy:
Well, God said, "Noah, there will be a
  flood,
But I'll keep you safe from the water and
  mud."
Noah listened to God, and his family was
  saved.

Al: Oh yeah!

Clyde: Oh yeah!

Elroy: Forty days and forty nights, the—

Al: Rain came falling down.

Hobart:
But because he listened to the Lord,
None of Noah's family drowned.
The ark settled down on Mount Ararat;
And we hope you've learned the simple
  lesson that—

Elroy: Noah listened to God and his family was saved.

Al: Oh yeah!

Clyde: Oh yeah!

All: OH YEAH!

LOST AND FOUND

Characters: **Harold**
Stella
Leader

(Before the skit begins, the leader should find a large, quartz-like stone and place it on the floor near the puppet stage.)

Harold *(excitedly)*: Oh boy, oh boy! I must have the best rock collection *anywhere*. I bet nobody else has as many pretty rocks as I do—especially now that I have that shiny new rock.

Stella *(entering)*: Oh, hi, Harold. What are you doing?

Harold: I'm on my way to look at my rock collection, Stella.

Stella: You collect *rocks?*

Harold: I sure do.

Stella: It figures. You're such a blockhead!

Harold: Oh, c'mon, Stella. Collecting rocks is a fun hobby.

Stella: What do you collect—diamonds, rubies, emeralds?

Harold: No, mostly just quartz, sandstone, and fool's gold.

Stella: *Fool's* gold, huh Harold? *(Turning to the* audience): I could say it, but I won't!

Harold: I do have some beautiful rocks, Stella. Especially the shiny new rock I found the other day.

Stella: Oh, could I see it, Harold, please?

Harold: Sure, Stella. I put it right over here.

(Moves over *and looks to the side.)* Or *(moves* to the *other side)* . . . maybe I put it over *here.* Oh, no, *Stella.* Oh, no! I *can't* find it! I've lost my shiny rock!

Stella *(impatiently)*: Well, *look* for it, silly. You must have put it someplace. Rocks don't just get up and walk away, you know.

Harold: I *am* looking, Stella, but I can't find it anywhere. *(He keeps looking from side to side.)*

Stella: Oh, Harold. Don't worry about it. It doesn't matter anyway. There are plenty more rocks in this world. Who cares if you lose just one?

Harold: *I* care, Stella. I really liked that rock.

Leader *(stepping up to the puppet stage)*: Hello, Harold and Stella. I overheard your conversation, and I thought maybe I could help.

Harold: Oh, I hope so, *(name).* I've lost my rock.

Stella *(sarcastically)*: He's lost his *marbles,* but there's nothing we can do about that!

Leader: Did you know that there's a chapter in the Bible where Jesus told three stories about things that were lost?

Harold: No, I didn't, *(name).* What chapter is that?

Leader: It's the fifteenth chapter of Luke. First, Jesus told about a man who had one hundred sheep and lost one of them.

Stella: Oh well, what's one sheep out of a hundred? He probably didn't even miss it.

Harold: But Stella, maybe that man felt about his sheep the same way I feel about my rock.

Leader: You're right, Harold. Jesus said the shepherd cared so much about his lost sheep that he went out to search for it. When he found it, he called together his friends and neighbors and they celebrated because he found the lost sheep.

Stella: Didn't Jesus tell another story about a lost coin?

Leader: That's right, Stella. Do you remember the story?

Stella: Well, a woman had ten coins and she lost one of them. So she lit up the house and swept the floor and searched until she found it.

Leader: That's right. And, like the shepherd, she called together her friends and neighbors and they celebrated that the lost coin had been found.

Harold: *(name)*, isn't there also a story about a lost son?

Leader: Yes there is, Harold. Sometimes he is called the "prodigal son."

Harold: Yeah, I remember the story. He went off to a distant land and wasted his money on wild living. When a famine came, he ended up hungry and poor. And he worked feeding pigs! Oink, oink!

Stella: We can do without the sound effects, Harold!

Harold: Anyway, he finally came to his senses and returned to his father.

Stella: Was his dad glad to see him again, Harold?

Harold: Sure. In fact, he threw a big party in his son's honor, because he was so happy to have him back.

Leader: Do you know what these stories teach us, Harold and Stella?

Stella: I'm not sure.

Harold: I know. They teach us that it feels bad to *lose* something and it feels good to *find* something.

Leader: That's true, Harold. But there's even more to it than that. Jesus told these stories to show how much God loves us, even though we have done bad things and have turned away from Him.

Stella: You mean, even with so many people in the world, God cares about each one of us?

Leader: That's right.

Harold: Just like, even with so many rocks in the world, I still want to find the one that's lost?

Leader: Right again. Jesus said, "There is joy before the angels of God when one sinner changes his heart" (Luke 15:10). That means that the angels celebrate when a lost person comes back to God!

Harold: Well, I have learned an important lesson today. *(Sadly)*: But I still can't find my pretty new rock.

Stella *(looking down at the floor)*: Hey, Harold, what's that on the floor?

Harold *(excitedly)*: It's my rock! *(Leader picks it up.)* Thanks, it must have fallen out of my pocket. Oh, goody! We've found my rock! We've found my rock!

Stella: But you've still lost your marbles! See you later, Harold. You, too, *(name)*.

Harold: Good-bye, Stella. Good-bye, *(name)*. *(They leave.)*

FEEDING THE FIVE THOUSAND

Characters: Leader
Harold

(Leader enters with a hot dog on a bun. Or, with a few minor changes in the script, a cookie or an apple can be substituted.)

Leader: Oh boy. I've got a real treat here, boys and girls: a nice warm hot dog on a bun. I'm really going to enjoy eating this hot dog.

Harold *(entering)*: Hi, *(name)*.

Leader: Oh, hi, Harold.

Harold: Boy, something sure smells good.

Leader: Oh, you probably smell this hot dog I'm getting ready to eat, Harold.

Harold: A hot dog? *(Leader nods.)* On a warm bun? With mustard? *(Leader nods again.)* With relish and pickles *(begins to talk faster and more excitedly)* and ketchup and sauerkraut and chili sauce and peanut butter?

Leader: Peanut butter on a hot dog? Oh, that doesn't sound very good to me, Harold. This is just an ordinary hot dog— but it's really going to taste good.

Harold: Well, *(name)*, I guess if you have only one hot dog, there's not enough for me to have a bite.

Leader: Well, as a matter of fact, Harold, I would be happy to give you part of my hot dog.

Harold *(surprised)*: You would?

Leader: Sure, Harold. Jesus wants us to share with others.

Harold: But if you give me part of the hot dog, then you won't have as much left to eat for yourself.

Leader: That's true. But it's funny, Harold. I've learned that when I trust in God and share generously with others, God always seems to provide all I really need for myself.

Harold: Hey, isn't there a story in the Bible about a little boy who shared his lunch with Jesus?

Leader: Yes, Harold. And Jesus used that little lunch to feed a big crowd of people.

Harold: Really? Say, *(name)*, would you tell me the story?

(Leader sings, "Feeding the Five Thousand," music on page 62.)

Verse 1:
    Well, there was one little boy,
        Five loaves of bread,
    Two fish to eat.
        Then Jesus said,
    "Oh, I will feed the multitude.
        All you have to do is trust in Me."

Verse 2:
    Well, there were five thousand men,
        Women, and kids.

No one could have guessed
    What Jesus did.
Oh, He fed the multitude.
    All they had to do was trust in Him.

Chorus:
    Jesus wants your all,
    Whether great or small.
    Jesus knows your heart.
    When you believe,
    You will receive
    Blessings that never depart.

(Harold and Leader repeat verses 1 and 2.)

Leader: Well, there was one little boy,

Harold: Five loaves of bread,

Leader: Two fish to eat.

Harold: Then Jesus said,

Both: "Oh, I will feed the multitude.
    All you have to do is trust in Me."

Harold: Well there were five thousand men,

Leader: Women, and kids.

Harold: No one could have guessed

Leader: What Jesus did.

Both: Oh, He fed the multitude.
    All they had to do was trust in Him.

Both: Oh, Jesus meets our ev'ry need;
    All we have to do is trust in Him.

Harold: Wow, that's a neat song.

Leader: And it's an important story, Harold.

Harold: Now, uh, not to be pushy or any-thing, but . . . could we eat the hot dog before it gets cold?

Leader: Sure, Harold. *(Breaks hot dog in two, places half in Harold's mouth. They both leave.)*

THE GOOD SAMARITAN

Characters:
>**Hobart the Worm**
>**Al the Gator**
>**Elroy Elephant the Third**
>**Harold**

Hobart (*entering*): Oh me, oh my! What a terrible day! (*Looks from side to side.*) Hey, where am I, anyway? Oh no! Here I am, out in the middle of nowhere. I'm *lost!* Where am I? (*Moans.*) Plus, I have an awful ache in my tummy! How's a worm supposed to crawl around with a sore tummy? Oh, I sure wish someone would help me find my way back home. (*Sadly*): I'm tired, I'm sore, and I'm *scared!*

(*Al the Gator enters.*)

Hobart: (*Looking at Al.*) Hey! There's Al the Gator! Hey, Mr. Gator! Could you please help me? I'm lost! I don't know how to get home. And I'm sick too. My tummy is so sore. (*Pleading*) Please . . . won't you help me?

Al: Uh . . . oh, hi, worm. Uh, you say you're lost, huh? Well, sorry. I'm late for my after-noon nap. I really need to go home *myself*, so I really can't help you. Sorry! (*Leaves.*)

Hobart: But Mr. Gator . . . oh, it's no use. (*Moans.*) Oh, I'm so miserable!

(*Elroy Elephant the Third enters.*)

Hobart: Oh! Mr. Elroy Elephant the Third! You'll help me, won't you? *Please!* You see, I'm lost, and I don't feel very well. I really need a friend right now.

Elroy: Oh, hi, worm. Oh my, you are quite a sad sight. Lost, you say? (*Hobart nods.*) And sick too? (*Hobart nods again.*) Does your stomach feel real tender and sore?

Hobart (*nodding*): Yes, it does.

Elroy: Do you have a tired, achy feeling in your head?

Hobart (*hopefully*): Yes, I do!

Elroy: Your tail is drooping, and you really need a friend?

Hobart (*with relief*): Oh, *yes*, Elroy! Have you felt the same way before?

Elroy (*abruptly*): No, as a matter of fact, I haven't!

Hobart (*disappointed*): *You* mean you won't help me?

Elroy: No, I couldn't do that. You see, I'm on my way to a football game, and I'm running a little late. I don't have time to help you right now. Sorry, worm. Maybe next time. (*Leaves.*)

Hobart: Oh, dear.

Elroy (*suddenly returning*): Hey, worm!

Hobart (*with renewed hope*): Yes, Elroy?

Elroy: Why don't you try some Rolaids for that stomach?

Hobart (*sadly*): OK, maybe I will. (*Elroy*

leaves.) Oh, what am I going to do? I feel so awful! *(Begins to cry.)*

(Harold enters.)

Harold: Why, it's Hobart the Worm! Hi, there! Oh! You're *crying.* What's the matter, Hobart?

Hobart: Oh, Harold! I feel miserable. I'm lost, and I'm sick, and I'm frightened. I just don't feel well at all!

Harold: Well, Hobart, ol' buddy, that's *terrible!* Here, I'll help you. *(Moves toward Hobart.)* Let's go back to my house, and I'll get you some nice hot food. My mom is frying some hamburgers. Then you can rest for a while so you will feel better.

Hobart: Oh, Harold, would you really do that?

Harold: Sure, Hobart! You could even take a nice warm bath. Just be careful—you're so long and skinny, you might go down the drain! Just kidding, Hobart!

Hobart: Oh, Harold, do you really want to help me?

Harold *(nodding)*: Of course I do! You're my neighbor, aren't you?

Hobart: Oh, thank you. You are such a wonderful friend. For a while there, I thought nobody cared. Oh, I'm so relieved.

Harold: Oh, I'm just glad I can help. You see, in Sunday school last week, we learned the story about the good Samaritan.

Hobart: The good Samaritan? What is that story about, anyway?

Harold: Well, it goes something like this.

(Harold sings "The Good Samaritan," music on page 66.)

A man was walking down the road
On his way to Jericho,
When all at once a band of robbers
Beat and robbed him, don't you know?

The man was left alone to die.
And then a certain priest passed by.
But tho' he saw the poor man's need,
He passed by on the other side.

And then a Levite passed that way.
He looked down where the poor man lay.
He just ignored the man because he
    thought
To help just wouldn't pay.

And soon there came another man.
He said, "I'll do the best I can."
And we can learn a special lesson from
The good Samaritan.

Yes, we can learn a special lesson from
The good Samaritan!

Hobart: Well, you sure are a good Samaritan, Harold! I appreciate all your help!

Harold: Anytime, Hobart, anytime.

DID YOU HEAR ME CRY?

Characters: Grandpa Gray
            Grandma Gray

(As Grandpa Gray enters, a puppeteer behind the stage holds up a photo album so it is visible to the audience. Grandpa looks at it.)

Grandpa *(sadly)*: Oh, boy, looking through the family photo album sure tugs at my heartstrings. There's my son on his first birthday. What a fine young man! And now he's grown up, with a life of his own. *(Begins to sniff.)* And there's my sweet little daughter, and all my grandchildren, and all my friends. *(Voice begins to crack.)* Oh, the Lord has blessed me through so many people. *(Sniffs, sputters.)* It's a bit more than a sentimental old fellow like me can hold in! *(Begins to cry.)*

Grandma *(enters, looks at Grandpa)*: Why, Grandpa Gray. What's the matter? Why are you crying?

(Grandpa sings "Did You Hear Me Cry?" music on page 68.)

Did you hear me cry?
Did you hear me sigh?
Don't you wonder why I'm crying?
My tears don't mean I'm sad;
And nothing's going bad.
It's just that all the years are flying.

The Lord has been so good to me.
He's always taken care of me,
And always helped me keep on trying.
And now I feel so thankful,
My eyes have got a "tank-full,"

And here I sit, just crying.
And here I sit, just crying.

Grandma: Why, Grandpa Gray, I don't think I've ever seen you cry so hard!

Grandpa *(sheepishly)*: Yeah, I know, Grandma. If this keeps up, I'm gonna have to go wring out my beard. It's getting wet!

Grandma: Oh Grandpa—

Grandpa: I'm ashamed, Grandma. A grown man like myself shouldn't sit around crying all the time.

Grandma: Well, Grandpa, you *don't* cry *all* the time. In fact, hardly ever. But now and then, there's nothing wrong with expressing your emotions. You just have a soft, loving heart, that's all.

Grandpa *(humorously)*: I also have a wet mustache! I think my nose is starting to run!

Grandma: Oh, Grandpa, when you look over a life as full as ours has been, you can't help but cry some tears of joy—and some tears of sadness that some happy stages of life are over. But, Honey, remember what the future has in store for us.

Grandpa: Right now, I'd settle for a handkerchief!

Grandma: Oh Grandpa!

Grandpa: Or a towel, maybe? My glasses are getting steamed up. *(Sniffs loudly.)*

And my nose is still running!

Grandma: Grandpa, it's all right to cry. The Bible says to weep with those who weep.

Grandpa: Right now, I could *drip* with those who *drip*, that's for sure!

Grandma: Grandpa, you know what I mean. Crying isn't a sign of weakness. We need to be tenderhearted, sympathetic, and willing to *feel* with one another.

Grandpa (*nodding*): You're right, Grandma. I remember reading in the Bible that even *Jesus* cried, when His friend Lazarus died.

Grandma (*nodding*): That's right, Grandpa. But don't forget, the Bible also says that in Heaven God will wipe away every tear from our eyes. There will be no more death, sadness, crying, or pain. (*See Revelation 21:4.*)

Grandpa: *Yes,* Grandma, in Heaven, there won't be any tears, because there won't be any *hurts*.

Grandma: Now, doesn't that make you feel better, Grandpa?

Grandpa (*nodding*): Yes, but (*pausing*) when I think how much God loves us, it makes me feel like crying. And I'm tired of having a wet beard!

Grandma: Well, wet beard or not, I love you, Grandpa Gray. (*She kisses him on the cheek, making a loud smacking noise.*)

Grandpa: Thank you, Sweetie. Your kisses still pack a wallop!

Grandma: Oh Grandpa, now I feel like crying.

(*They sing reprise of "Did You Hear Me Cry?"*)

He: Did you hear me cry?

Grandma: Yes, I heard you cry.

Both: And we both know why we're crying.

He: Our love throughout the years,

She: Our problems and our fears,

Both: Have blended into joy abiding.

He: With Jesus as our Lord and King,

She: With loved ones near who laugh and sing,

Both:
We will always keep on trying.
And now we feel so thankful,
Our eyes have got a "tank-full,"
And here we sit, just crying.
And here we sit, just crying.

He: Did you hear me cry?

She: Yes, I heard you cry.

Both: And we both know why we're crying.

COME TO VBS

Characters: Kenny Cool
Clyde the Dog

(This skit is good to use for a VBS pre-registration day or on the first day of Vacation Bible School to promote attendance.)

Kenny *(entering)*: *Hey, boys* and girls, have I got some news for you! *(Excitedly)*: Guess what's coming up on *(date)*? We're going to have Vacation Bible School! Man, it makes me feel like *singing!*

Clyde *(entering)*: Woof, woof! Hello, Kenny. Hello, boys and girls. Woof, woof! What are you so excited about, Kenny?

Kenny: You mean you haven't heard, Clyde? Hey, get with it, man! Vacation Bible school is comin' our way 'most any day!

Clyde: Vacation Bible School? Oh, I love Vacation Bible School!

Kenny: Me too, Clyde. In fact, it makes me feel like singing!

Clyde: Mind if I join you, Kenny? I love to sing too. Woof, woof!

Kenny: I don't mind, Clyde. Go ahead and make some notes with your throat, man!

(They sing "Come to VBS," page 73.)

Chorus:
Both: Come to VB, come to VB, Come to VBS!
Clyde: Oh, yes, oh, yes, it's VBS!

Both: Come to VB, Come to VB, Come to VBS!

Clyde: Oh, *yes,* oh, *yes,* it's VBS!

Verse 1:
Kenny:
It's that time of the year.
The summer is here,
The public schools are out.
We want something to do.
That's special and new.
We need it now,
There is no doubt.

Where can we go
Where we'll have lots of fun,
Where we'll sing
And we'll laugh,
And we'll see ev'ryone?

(Repeat chorus.)

Kenny:
It's a place where we sing
About Jesus our King.
We learn about God's Son.
We make so many crafts,
And we have lots of laughs.
.It's so much fun for everyone!

Where do you go
If you wanna be cool?
The place you should be
Is vacation Bible school!

(Repeat chorus. After last chorus sing):

Come and see me,
Don't say maybe,
Come to VBS!
Come to VBS!
YES!

DISCOVERY

Characters: Bernadette
Barney

(Bernadette enters with a baby in her arms—a doll wrapped in a blanket, pinned or taped to her arms.)

Bernadette *(lovingly)*: Oh, I just can't believe it's true. My very own, brand new baby brother! Oh, Sheldon, you're so cute. You're so tiny! Look at those perfect little fingers and those precious little blue eyes.

Barney *(entering)*: Uh, hi, Bernadette. Uh, who are you talking to?

Bernadette: Oh, Barney, this is my brand new baby brother. His name is Sheldon. Isn't he adorable?

Barney: Yeah, he's cute. And boy! Is he *little!* How old is he, anyway?

Bernadette: He's just three weeks old, Barney.

Barney: Three weeks? Is that less than one year?

Bernadette: Yep! He's not even one yet.

Barney *(surprised)*: You mean he's *zero?*

Bernadette: I guess you could say that, Barney.

Barney: Wow! I never heard of that before! What does He *do,* anyway?

Bernadette: Well, he doesn't do too much. He just eats and sleeps all the time.

Barney: Boy, that sounds just like *(name a person in the audience).*

Bernadette: You see, Barney, Sheldon doesn't know anything—

Barney: Now that *really* sounds like *(repeats name of person in the audience).*

Bernadette: Barney, as Sheldon's older sister, I'm going to do my best to teach him all about the world around him.

Barney: That's going to be a big job, Bernadette.

Bernadette: Oh, I know, Barney. There's just so much to learn!

Barney: There sure is. Uh-oh! I think I hear my mother calling. I'd better go now. Thanks for showing me your cute little baby brother. Good-bye, Bernadette. *(He leaves.)*

Bernadette *(thoughtfully)*: Oh, Sheldon. There is so much to learn and discover.

(She sweetly and thoughtfully sings, "Discovery," words and music on page 77.)

Verse 1, chorus
Verse 2, chorus
Verse 3

Bernadette *(softly)*: Good-night, Sheldon. And sweet dreams!

I'M SO ANGRY

Characters: Stella
Harold

(As Stella enters, a puppeteer behind the stage holds up an open Bible so it is visible to the audience. Stella looks at it.)

Stella *(angrily)*: Oh, brother! Where is that verse, anyway? Wouldn't you know? I can't even find it.

Harold *(enters, speaking cheerfully)*: Oh, boy, what a nice day!

Stella *(loudly)*: No, it isn't. It's an *awful* day! And it's all your fault, Harold!

Harold: *My* fault? Why? What did I do, Stella?

Stella: You were *born*, that's what, Harold. All of my problems are your fault and everybody else's fault too.

Harold: What kind of problems are you talking about, Stella?

Stella: Well, for one thing, I can't find the Bible verse our Sunday School teacher wanted us to read.

Harold: Well, calm down, Stella. It's not your teacher's fault, you know.

Stella: Plus, you know that job I had—baby-sitting for the Smiths? *(Harold nods.)* Well, they *fired* me today, just because I didn't show up for two measly weeks in a row.

Harold: You were supposed to baby-sit, and you didn't show up for *two* weeks, Stella?

Stella: Yes, I had other things to do—my nails, my hair, my eyes.

Harold: What did you do to your eyes?

Stella: I *closed* them, silly. I love to sleep, you know.

Harold: But Stella, I don't *blame* the Smiths for firing you if you didn't show up for work.

Stella: Oh, nonsense, Harold. It's all their fault. Plus, today my little brother spilled ink on my best dress.

Harold: But Stella, I heard your mom tell you not to leave your bottle of ink out where your brother could get it.

Stella: Oh, Harold, all I know is—lots of things have gone wrong today, and *none* of it—NONE OF IT—has been my fault!

(Sings, "I'm So Angry" page 80.)

I'm so angry! I'm so mad!
This is the worst day I've ever had!
I should have known it was a warning
When I burned the toast this morning,
And I stubbed my toe when I got out of
    bed.

I'm so angry! I'm so peeved!
And things are worse than you'd believe.
So I'll yell at the dog and fuss at the cat,
And step on my little brother's hat,
And I'll slam the door quite loudly when I
    leave!
(Speaking rhythmically): I'm so mad.

30

Harold: But Stella!

Stella: It's not my fault.

Harold: But Stella!

Stella: It's a shame,

Harold: I'm trying to tell her—

Stella: But *others* are to blame.

Harold: But *Stella! (Sings)*:

I know you're angry, I know you're mad.
And it's the worst day you've ever had.
But instead of blaming everyone else,
Why don't you humbly look at yourself?
And see if there's *some* truth in what *I've*
said.

I know you're angry; I know you're tired.
But some insight is required.
Don't blame everyone else for things
you've done.
By passing the buck, you ruin the fun.
(Sighs.)
But I've probably said much more than
you desired.

(Spoken rhythmically):

Stella: I hate to admit it.

Harold: Yes, Stella?

Stella: But you're right!

Harold: *Really,* Stella?

Stella: You've pointed out, you see, My
responsibility.

Harold: Oh, yeah.

Stella *(with conviction)*: I need to forgive
the faults of others, as God has forgiven
me.

(They sing):

Stella: I'm not so angry anymore.

Harold: She's not so angry anymore.

Stella: And I'm sorry I've been a bore.

Harold: And she's sorry she's been a bore.
Others' faults are always easy to see,

Stella: But it's harder to see the faults in
me.

Together:
But we're going to do much better, you
will see.
Yes, we're going to do much better, you
will see!
You will see, you will see.

Harold: See you, Stella. *(Leaves.)*

Stella: Good-bye, Harold. *(Glances down at
her open Bible.)* Well, what do you know?
Here's that Bible verse I was looking for:
James 4:1. *(Reads verse from Bible)*: "Do
you know where your fights and arguments
come from? They come from the selfish
desires that make war inside you." *(Looking
up.)* You're right, Lord, You're right.

31

"I" TROUBLE

Characters: Harold
Three Sock Puppets:
I, Me, Myself

(See instructions for making the sock puppets on page 110.)

(I, Me, and Myself enter, one at a time. Each has his name pinned on his chest. Then Harold enters.)

Harold: Dum, de-dum, dum-dum. *(Notices the other puppets.)* Oh, hi, there! Who are you?

I: I'm I.

Me: I'm Me.

Myself: I'm Myself.

Harold: Oh, yeah? You guys just look like plain old sock puppets to me.

Me: Are you making fun of me?

Myself: I was wondering that *myself!*

I: I am sure he is putting us down. And I am usually *right!*

Harold: No, fellows. I wasn't putting you down. Really, I *like* sock puppets. In fact, I'd like to get acquainted with you guys. OK?

I: I guess so.

Me: It's all right with me.

Myself: I don't mind, if I say so *myself.*

Harold *(pausing, as if trying to think of something to say)*: Uh . . . so . . . how *are* you guys today?

I: I'm fine.

Me: Me too.

Myself: I'm really not feeling like myself today.

Harold: Why not?

Me: *He's* probably jealous of *me!*

I: I think he has an I-dentity problem, that's what I think.

Harold: *Hey,* wait a minute. Why don't you guys let Myself speak for himself?

Myself: I was wondering that *myself!*

I: Because I want you to pay attention to me.

Me: Thanks.

I: No, I mean *I* want all the attention.

Harold: But wait a minute. Myself needs some encouragement. Who is going to help *him?*

I: Not I! I can't help Myself!

Me: Don't look at *me!*

Harold: Then I'll just help Myself *myself.* Why don't you feel like yourself, Myself?

(Looks at the audience and sighs.)

Myself: Because no one will let me just be *myself!*

I: I will let you be yourself.

Me: Sure. It doesn't bother me.

Myself: I've convinced myself that you guys are too self-centered to care about me.

Me: Well I certainly care about me!

I *(sarcastically)*: You would.

Harold: Wait a minute, fellas, wait a minute. Why are you arguing among yourselves?

Myself: I was wondering that *myself.*

I: This isn't an argument. I just happen to be *right.*

Me: You could have fooled me.

Harold: All I know is, all three of you seem much too concerned about yourselves, and not *nearly* concerned enough about *others.*

Myself: *Myself* . . . well, I'm afraid you may be right.

Me: *Me* too.

I: I see your point.

Harold: Philippians 2:3, 4 says, "When you do things, do not let selfishness or pride be your guide. Be humble and give more honor to others than to yourselves. Do not be interested only in your own life, but be interested in the lives of others."

I: But what can I do?

Me: And what about me?

Myself: How can I stop being so preoccupied with *myself?*

Harold: It's not easy, fellows. We all have an ego, a desire to put ourselves first. But in Mark 8:34, Jesus said, "If anyone wants to follow me, he must say 'no' to the things he wants."

I: I wonder what it means to say no to the things I want?

Harold: It means that if we want things that will keep us from getting close to Jesus, we have to say "no" to those things.

Me: It seems to me that *Jesus* should be first in our lives.

Harold: That's right. Let me explain it this way.

(Sings "Jesus and Me," page 87.)

Verse 1:
  Jesus and me
  Eternally,
  He is my Lord, and He always will be.
  I'm bound to the One from Galilee.
  Jesus and me
  Submissively,
  I am His servant,
  and I always will be.
  I've found serving Him is liberty.

Chorus:
  He is why I am happy.
(Sock puppets sing): "Why I am happy.")
  He is why I am free.
(Sock puppets sing): "Why I am free.")
  He is why I have so much to live for.
  He is my King and I will sing of Jesus and
    me.

Verse 2:
Jesus and me
Positively,
Life's in my future, and it always will be.
I've frowned, but He brings a smile to me.
Jesus and me
So lovingly,
He brought salvation to a sinner like me.
I'm grounded on His Word so solidly.

(Repeat chorus. After last chorus sing):

Jesus and me
Eternally,
He is my Lord,
and He always will be.
Jesus, Jesus, Jesus—Jesus and me!

Myself: Well, I myself can't argue with that!

I: I've learned *my* lesson. Now I really must be going.

Me: Me, too. *(I and Me leave.)*

Harold *(notices they are gone, then looks at Myself)*: Well, I guess I'll just sit around and talk to *Myself* for a while! Ha, ha! Get it? I'm just going to sit around and talk to Myself!

Myself: I couldn't have said it better *myself!*

I LOVE MY SUNDAY SCHOOL

Characters: Kenny Cool
              Barney

(This skit is good to use during a Sunday-school opening or some other occasion when Sunday school needs to be emphasized.)

Kenny *(entering)*: Cool, man! What a sharp-looking bunch of boys and girls. I mean, you're really with it! *(Moves briskly back and forth across the stage.)* I can tell you are the kind of kids that would really like Sunday school. I mean, it's cool to like Sunday school! I like Sunday school, and I'm the coolest dude around!

(Sings "I Love My Sunday School," words and music on page 92.)

Barney *(entering)*: Uh, hi, Kenny. Uh, what's this you're saying? Sunday school is cool?

Kenny *(nodding)*: That's right, Barney old boy. It's cool, man, real cool!

Barney: So why don't they turn up the furnace a little bit?

Kenny: No, Barney, I mean Sunday school is fun, it's groovy, it's right on! Do you go to Sunday school, Barney?

Barney: Uh, well, sometimes I do. But usually I sleep late and I don't make it.

Kenny: Hey, you want to hit me with that again, man?

Barney: I didn't hit you!

Kenny: No, I mean *say* it again—that last part about the sleeping.

Barney: I said, usually I sleep late and I don't make it.

Kenny: Hey, man. Get *with* it! Sunday school is the place to be on Sunday morning! I wouldn't miss it for anything! It's *numero uno* on my list!

Barney: Numero what-o?

Kenny: Numero *uno*, Barney! You know—number one! *Nothing* crowds out my Sunday school.

Barney: Uh, well, I never realized Sunday school was that much fun.

Kenny: You'd better believe it, Barney. Man, you should hear the Bible stories!.

Barney: They're really exciting?

Kenny *(nodding)*: You'd better believe it! Stories about the most exciting things that have ever happened on earth are in the Bible!

Barney *(wistfully)*: Wow. What else do you do in Sunday school?

Kenny: We sing some really neat songs! And sometimes act out a story, or make crafts, or ask our teacher about a problem, or talk with our friends.

Barney: Well, Kenny, you've talked me into it. From now on, I'm going to Sunday school *every* Sunday!

Kenny: Now you're talkin'! And hey, man, don't forget to bring a friend!*(Sings.)*
    My name is Kenny, and I'm cool.
    I love my Sunday school! Yeah!

A CHRISTMAS POEM

Characters: Stella
Harold
Bernadette
Grandpa Gray

Harold (enters muttering): Let's see . . . "Christmas is a time for song . . ."

Stella (enters humming, "Jingle Bells"): Oh, hi, Harold. What are you doing?

Harold: I'm working on a Christmas poem, Stella. I thought I would write a nice poem, put it on a Christmas card I made myself, and give it to my mother and dad for their present this year.

Stella: That sounds like a *great* idea, Harold. So what's the problem?

Harold: I just can't get the words to rhyme, Stella.

Stella: Rhyme? Oh, Harold, rhymes are easy. I do rhymes *lots* of times! You have to know 'em to write a poem! See how easy it is, Harold?

Harold: Well, maybe it's easy for you, but it's not easy for *me*.

Bernadette (entering): Hi, Harold and Stella. How's your poem going, Harold?

Harold: I have a problem, Bernadette. I just can't get the words to *rhyme*.

Bernadette: Like I always say, Harold, if you can't rhyme the *words*, then your poem's for the *birds*!

Stella (laughing): Hey, that's pretty good, Bernadette!

Harold (sarcastically): Yeah, thanks for the encouragement, Bernadette. You girls are no help at all!

Stella: Well, here comes Grandpa Gray. Maybe *he* can help you write your poem, Harold.

(Grandpa Gray enters, coughing.)

Harold: Hi, Grandpa Gray. Boy, it sounds like you have a bad cold, Grandpa.

Grandpa (cough, cough): Yes, I most certainly do, Harold. (Sputter, cough) Christmas is a *terrible* time to have a cold!

Bernadette: Grandpa, we were trying to help Harold write a Christmas poem for his mother and dad. Do you think you could help?

Grandpa: Ahem (cough, cough). Well, I'll try. (Nods.) I have always been pretty good with rhymes.

Stella: Well, Harold, why don't you read part of the poem? We'll help you with the trouble spots.

Harold: OK. There's one part about how Jesus Christ was born in the town of Beth . . . what was the name of that town . . . Beth—?

Grandpa (coughing): Ahem.

Stella: Was it Jerusalem?

Harold: No, I'm sure it was Beth something.

Grandpa (coughing louder): Ahem!

Bernadette: I know. It was the town of *Bethany.*

Harold: No, that's not it. Let's see . . . Beth . . . Beth—

Grandpa (loudly): AHEM!

Harold (finally noticing Grandpa): That's it, Grandpa Gray! (Excitedly): *Bethlehem!* Hey, now we're getting somewhere.

Stella: Did you need help with any of the *other* lines, Harold?

Harold: Well, listen to this one:
"The message still is thrilling news,
And true in every season.
Its joy is there for men to—"

Stella: I've got it! "Its joy is there for men to *pick.*"

Grandpa (beginning to sneeze): Ah— Ah—

Harold: No, Stella, it has to rhyme with "news."

Bernadette: I've got it. "Its joy is there for men to *confuse.*"

Grandpa (louder, still on the verge of sneezing): Ah— Ah—

Harold: No, Bernadette, there has to be a better word than that.

Grandpa: AH— AH— AH—.

Harold: "The message still is thrilling news,
And true in every season.
Its joy is there for men to

Grandpa (sneezing): CHOOOOO!!!!

Harold: CHOOSE! That's it! (Excitedly): "Its joy is there for men to *choose.*" Grandpa Gray, you've done it again!

Grandpa (sniffing, sputtering): Why, think nothing of it, Harold.

Stella: So, is your poem finished now, Harold?

Harold: Yes, it is, Stella. And I was wondering . . . would the three of you like to help me read it?

Bernadette: Sure! We'd be honored, wouldn't we?

Stella (nodding eagerly): We sure would!

Grandpa (sniffs, coughs): Well, this cough hasn't stolen all my Christmas cheer! I'll be happy to join in.

Harold: OK, then. Stella, you go first.

Stella: Christmas is a time for song,

Harold: A time for words of cheer;

Bernadette: A time for feeling you belong

Grandpa: With friends and family dear.

Stella: Christmas is a time for treats

Harold: And giving Christmas presents;

Bernadette: A time for trees and lights and sweets

Grandpa: And glowing fires so pleasant.

Stella: Christmas is a time for joy,

Harold: A time for fun and mirth;

Bernadette: But most of all a time to think

Grandpa: About the Savior's birth.

Stella: God sent His Son to live on earth

Harold: In spite of all the danger.

Bernadette: A humble virgin gave Him birth

Grandpa: And laid Him in a manger.

Stella: Angels came to shepherds then

Harold: With glorious news to tell to them:

Bernadette: That Jesus Christ was born that day

Grandpa: In the town of Beth-AHEM!

Stella: The greatest Christmas gift of all

Harold: Is the One God freely gave us.

Bernadette: For young and old and big and small,

Grandpa: God sent His Son to save us.

Stella: The message still is thrilling news

Harold: And true in every season.

Bernadette: Its joy is there for men to choose,

Grandpa: And Jesus is the reason!

Harold: Merry Christmas, everyone!

Grandpa: And to all a— *(Begins to sneeze again.)* Ah— Ah— AH—

Stella, Harold, and **Bernadette** *(finishing it for Grandpa)*: And to all a good night!

Grandpa: CHOOOO!!!!

I AM THANKFUL

Characters: Stella
Bernadette
Harold
Barney

Stella, Bernadette, and Harold (*singing*):
Happy birthday to you,
Happy birthday to you,
Happy birthday dear Barney,
Happy birthday to you!

(*They cheer*): Hooray for Barney!

Barney (*impatiently*): All right, knock it off everybody! Let's hurry up and eat the cake.

Bernadette: Now Barney, don't be so impatient! We were just singing happy birthday to you.

Barney: Big deal! Hurry up and cut the cake! I'm hungry!

Stella: Boy, what a grouch.

Harold: Hey, Barney, did you notice that your mother baked your favorite kind of cake—chocolate cake with white icing?

Barney: Yeah, I noticed. C'mon, let's eat.

Stella: And she even decorated it in a real special way.

Harold: Yeah! She knows you like baseball, Barney, so she took green icing and made a baseball field on top of the cake. It has an infield, bases, a pitcher's mound, and everything!

Bernadette: Wow, Barney, it must have taken her hours to make that cake. I hope you thanked your mother for all her work, Barney.

Barney (*still impatient*): Thank her? No way! She didn't need to go to all that work. Any old cake will do when you're hungry.

Stella: Hey, Barney, isn't it neat? Your dad gave you a red wagon for your birthday!

Harold: Yeah, and he made it himself! He built the wagon out in the garage late at night while you were sleeping, Barney.

Bernadette: And he painted it red.

Barney (*bluntly*): I know! When I saw the wagon, I told him I would rather have had a blue one.

Harold (*slowly*): Uh, Barney . . . you mean you didn't say "thank you" to your dad for building that wagon?

Barney (*matter-of-factly*): Nope. Why should I? It isn't even my favorite color.

Stella (*with irritation*): What about all the birthday gifts your friends gave you, Barney? What about this great party? Aren't you going to say, "thank you" to any of them for the nice things they've done for you?

Barney: As a matter of fact, Stella—NO!

Bernadette (*disgusted*): Well! I have never

seen such a bad attitude!

Stella: C'mon, Bernadette. Let's go skating.

Bernadette: All right. See you later, Harold. And Barney— happy birthday . . . I guess.

(Stella and Bernadette leave.)

Barney: Hey, Harold, I think those girls were *angry* with me.

Harold: Yes, Barney. *(Nods.)* I think you're right!

Barney: But why, Harold?

Harold: Because they think you should be more thankful for all the nice things people have done for you. And you know what, Barney?

Barney: What, Harold?

Harold: I think they're *right!* Barney, we shouldn't take it for granted when people do nice things for us. We should thank them. We should thank *God.* We should appreciate things more, and we should say those words, "I am thankful," a lot more often!

(Harold sings, "I Am Thankful," music on page 95.)

I am thankful for the fun I've had,
I'm thankful for my mom and dad,
I'm thankful for the things I hope to be.

I am thankful for my God above,
I'm thankful for His matchless love,
I'm thankful for all He's done for me.

Joy to share with friends,
A hope that never ends,
Encouragement when I'm down;
The promises of God—those words that
ring so true;
Blessings like these are accepted with
ease,
But there's one thing I must do:
I'll be thankful, so very thankful.

(Harold and Barney sing):

We are thankful for the fun we've had,
We're thankful for our moms and dads,
We're thankful for the things we hope to
be.

We are thankful for our God above,
We're thankful for His matchless love,

Barney *(singing alone)*: I'm thankful for all He's done for me.

Barney *(slowly)*: Hey, uh, Harold . . . why don't we eat that birthday cake later? Right now, I want to go say "Thank you" to my mother and dad and to all my friends.

Harold: OK, see you later, Barney!

Barney: And, Harold . . . thanks!

WHY IN THE WORLD?

Characters: Harold
                Stella

(Harold and Stella enter.)

Harold: Hey Stella, did you hear the news?

Stella: News? What news? *(Excitedly)*: Oh! I just love to hear the latest stuff!

Harold: Well Stella, I'm trying to tell you—

Stella *(interrupting)*: Let me guess! I know—you got in trouble at school and your parents grounded you for a whole month!

Harold *(shaking his head)*: No, Stella, it's nothing like that.

Stella: Humm . . . I know! You're having a big pizza party at your house and you're inviting all your friends! Remember Harold, I like lots of pepperoni!

Harold: No, Stella. The news isn't about a pizza party.

Stella *(thoughtfully)*: Oh, now I've got it! It's that cute new guy in our youth group—he has a crush on me, doesn't he?

Harold: No.

Stella *(disappointed)*: No? He doesn't like me?

Harold *(growing impatient, raising his voice)*: Stella, the news has nothing to do with your boyfriends!

Stella *(also growing impatient, raising her voice)*: Then *what in the world* is this important news you have to tell me?

Harold: It's about our youth minister.

Stella: Our youth minister? Oh, he's such a great guy. I really like him. In fact, everybody in our church likes him.

Harold: Well, Stella, he's going to be leaving us in a couple of months.

Stella *(surprised)*: Leaving? Oh no! He can't leave! I love our youth minister! What will we do without him? Who will lead our Bible Bowl team?

Harold *(trying to interrupt her)*: Stella—

Stella *(talking rapidly)*: Who will be there when we need somebody to talk to about a problem at school? Who will organize our lock-ins?

Harold: Stella—

Stella: Who will teach our Bible study? Who will take us on mission trips, and make our parties lots of fun?

Harold: STELLA! Calm down and listen, will you?

Stella: *(more calmly, and with sadness)*: Sorry, Harold. I just don't understand.

Harold: I feel sad too, Stella. But wait 'til you hear what our youth minister is going to be doing when he leaves!

Stella: Well, whatever he does, it certainly can't be as important as staying here with us! *Why in the world* is he leaving? *Why in the world* would he just pick up and move, right when we were all getting to know him so well? *Why in the world*?

Harold: Actually, "why in the world" is a good way to say it, Stella. *(Seriously)*: You see, he's going to be a missionary.

Stella *(surprised)*: A missionary? *Why in the world* would he want to do that?

Harold: There you go again, Stella. "Why in the world" is just the point! God loves the whole world, and wants everyone to hear about His love. And Jesus said to go into all the world and make disciples. That what our youth minister is going to do.

Stella: But don't we need to make disciples right here in our own neighborhood?

Harold *(nodding)*: Yes, of course! But somebody needs to be willing to go to other places to tell those people about Jesus.

Stella: Well, couldn't we just send some money? Why do we have to give up our youth minister?

Harold *(thoughtfully)*: Humm . . . Jesus did say it's more blessed to give than to receive. But we need to give more than just our money. We need to give our time, our talents—

Stella *(slowly)*: And maybe sometimes, we even need to give our friends—like our youth minister.

Harold: That's right, Stella. We're going to miss him, but won't it be great to have someone we know and love serving the Lord in another part of the world?

Stella *(more excitedly)*: You're right, Harold! Maybe our youth group could give him a big going-away party!

Harold: And we could pray for him.

Stella: And we can send letters and cards to encourage him. And maybe someday we could even go visit him on the mission field!

Harold: Why, Stella, *(with emphasis and a bit of sarcasm)*: *Why in the world* would someone like you consider leaving here and going to another part of the world?

Stella: Because I want all the people, in every nation, to know about the Lord!

(They sing, "See His Glory," music on page 99.)

Chorus

Harold: The Lord God reigns, let the earth be glad—

Stella: Let all the people see His glory.

Harold: The heavens proclaim His righteousness—

Stella: Let all the people see His glory.

Harold: He created the earth by His mighty hand—

Stella: Let all the people see His glory.

Harold: Then He came to earth and He lived as a man.

Stella: Let all the people see His glory. (Repeat chorus.)

Stella: He lived, He died, and He rose for me—

Harold: Let all the people see His glory.

Stella: He's the King of kings for eternity.

Harold: Let all the people see His glory.

(Repeat chorus, have children join in on the line, "Let all the people see His glory.")

ALL YEAR 'ROUND

Written by David and Candy Faust
Arranged by Penny Faust

Harold

In the win - ter I'm a

Stella ... Harold

win - ner. In the spring - time I can sing la - la - la! In the

to Coda

Both

sum - mer I'm a be - com - er, ___ And in the au - tumn up and at 'em with a

zing! All year round, we

bring all our days to the Lord. ___ All year

round, we sing and give praise to the Lord! In the

Harold

Stella

win - ter I'm a win - ner; ___ In the spring-time rob - ins call. In the

44

Harold

sum - mer I re - mem - ber, ____ that in the au - tumn I'll nev - er

fall.   (Spoken: Ha, ha... get it?   "In the *autumn* I'll never *fall*"... ha, ha, ha!)

Both

All   year   round,   we   bring   all our days   to the

Lord. ____   All   year   round,   we

45

D.S. al Coda

Harold **✛ CODA**

Both

sing   and give praise   to the   Lord!   In the   *zing!*   In the

au - tumn,   up and at   'em;   In the   au - tumn,   up and

at   'em;   In the   au - tumn,   up and   at   'em   with a

zing!

46

THE VERY WORRIED WORM

Written by David and Candy Faust
Arranged by Penny Faust

47

wor-ried a-bout,   here's what I'm wor-ried a-bout:

What if I tried to dig a hole and found I'd on-ly fail?
What if I had a gar-den and my plants just would-n't grow?

What if a wan-d'ring walk-er slipped and stepped up-on my tail?
What if the win-ter came and I was bur-ied in the snow?

What if I were the cap-tain of a ship that would-n't sail?
What if I threw a par-ty and my friends just did-n't show?

D.S. al Coda
These are the things I am wor-ried a-bout! I'm a
CODA
I'm a woe-ful, wish-y, wash-y, wor-ried worm.
Hobart sings
I will learn to be con-tent, and wor-ries I'll
do with-out; Wor-ries I'll do with-out, wor-ries I'll

do with-out.   For as long as God is with me, sure-ly I

should-n't doubt;   Wor-ries I'll do with-out, what should I

wor-ry a-bout?   And so if I trust the Lord to see me

through each pass - ing day;   And if I fill my time with whole-some

work and whole-some play; And if I learn to serve the Lord in

what I do and say, These health - y things will crowd the

Grandpa sings harmony

wor - ry out! We will learn to be con-tent, and wor-ries we'll

do with-out, Wor-ries we'll do with-out, wor-ries we'll

do with-out. For as long as God is with us, sure-ly we

should -n't doubt; Wor-ries we'll do with-out, what should we

wor -ry a-bout? For as long as God is with us, sure-ly we

rit. Hobart finishes alone   *a tempo*

should -n't doubt. I'm a wor-ry-free, a won-der-f'ly wis - er worm!

rit.   *a tempo*

AL THE GATOR

Written by David and Candy Faust
Arranged by Penny Faust

Al sings *lazily*

I'm a 'ga-tor, _____ "Al __ the

Ga - tor" ____ And I'd rath - er meet-cha now than

la - ter. __ 'Cause la - ter on I'll be nap-ping 'neath a tree, and I

don't need a pesk - y ag - gra - va - tor! __ I'm a

'ga - tor, _____ "Al __ the Ga - tor" _____ And I
And I'd

love to sleep, there's noth - ing great - er. _____ But
rath - er meet - cha now than la - ter. _____ I'm a

I'll wake up, you see, when some - one brings to me a
la - zy guy, you see I'd be

scrump - tious meal served by a fan - cy wait - er! __ I'm a

54

cra - zy not to be, 'cause the la - zy life's the on - ly life for

me! (Yawns)

Script, then Reprise   Hobart - Al sing

I'm a

'ga - tor_____ "Al the Ga - tor"_____   'Guess I
And I've

had to learn it soon - er or la - ter;_____   That
nev - er known a 'ga - tor who was great - er._____   From

55

la - zi - ness, you see, is not so good for me. As a
now on you will see, I'll be bus - y as a bee.

friend in - deed, I'm not a hes - i - tat - or! You're a

2. 'Cause the bus - y life's the on - ly life for me! Yes, a

bus - y life's the on - ly life for me!

J-E-S-U-S

Written by David and Candy Faust
Arranged by J. Anderson

J - E - S-U-S, Je - sus is the ver-y__ best.__ He brought

last time, to 3rd ending

1.

peace, joy, a love that's true— Je - sus can be your__ friend, too.

58

NOAH'S ARK

Written by David and Candy Faust
Arranged by Penny Faust

Elroy sings

Al sings

1. El - e - phants and worms and dogs — al - li - ga - tors,
2. Wal - rus - es and por - cu - pines and hop - ping kan ga -
3. For - ty days and for - ty nights, the rain came fall - ing

Hobart sings

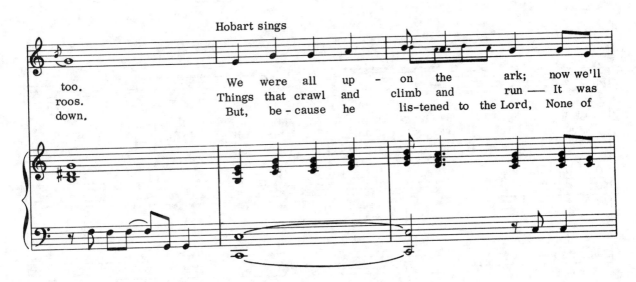

too.
roos.
down.

We were all up - on the ark; now we'll
Things that crawl and climb and run — It was
But, be - cause he lis - tened to the Lord, None of

59

tell   that   sto - ry   to   you.   Well,
real - ly   quite___ a   zoo!   Well,
No - ah's   fam - i - ly   drowned.   The

God   said,   "No - ah, bet - ter   build a_____ boat.   If you
God   said,   "No - ah, there will   be a_____ flood,   but I'll
ark   set - tled down on Mount   Ar - a - rat;   and we

don't,   you're   nev - er gon - na   stay a - float."__
keep   you   safe   from the   water and   mud."__
hope   you've   learn'd the sim - ple   les - son   that ___

60

FEEDING THE FIVE THOUSAND

Written by David and Candy Faust
Arranged by Penny Faust

Well, there was one lit - tle boy,
five thou-sand men,

Five loaves of bread,
wom - en and kids.

Two fish to eat.
No one could have guessed

Then Je - sus said, "Oh,
what Je - sus did. Oh,

I will feed the mul - ti - tude.
He___ fed the mul - ti - tude.

All you have to do is trust in
All they had to do was trust in

62

me._____ Well, there were Him._____

Je-sus wants your all wheth-er great or small. Je - sus knows your

8 -

heart.__ When you be-lieve, you will re-ceive

63

bles - sings that nev — er de - part! Well, there was

one lit - tle boy, five loaves of bread, Two fish to eat.
five thou-sand men, wom - en and kids. No one could have guessed

Then Je - sus said, "Oh, I will feed the mul - ti - tude.
what Je - sus did. Oh, He____ fed the mul - ti - tude.

65

THE GOOD SAMARITAN

Written by David and Candy Faust
Arranged by Penny Faust

Harold sings

A man was

walk - ing down the ro - ad on his way to Jer - i - cho, When all at
left a - lone to die. And then a cer - tain priest passed by. But tho' he

1.

once a band of rob - bers beat and robbed him, don't you know? The man was
saw the poor man's need,

2.

rit.   *a tempo*

He passed by on the oth - er side. And then a

rit.   *a tempo*

Le - vite passed that way. He looked down where the poor man lay. He just ig -
came an - oth - er man. He said, "I'll do the best I can." And we can

nored the man be - cause he tho't to help just would - n't pay. And soon there
learn a spe - cial les -

son from the good Sam - a - ri - tan. Yes, we can

learn a spe - cial les - son from the good Sam - a - ri - tan. _____

DID YOU HEAR ME CRY?

Written by David and Candy Faust
Arranged by Penny Faust

Grandpa Gray sings

Did you hear me cry? Did you hear me sigh?

flowing

Don't you won der why I'm cry - ing? My

tears don't mean I'm sad; And noth-ing's go - ing bad. It's

just that all the years are fly — ing. The

Lord has been so good to me. He's al – ways tak – en care of me, And

al – ways help'd me keep on try – ing. And

now I feel so thank-ful, my eyes have got a "tank-full," and

here I ___ sit, just cry - ing. And

here I sit, just cry - ing.

Grandpa   Grandma

Did you hear me cry?   Yes, I heard you cry.

flowing

Both   Grandpa

And we both know why we're cry - ing. Our

now we feel so thank-ful,   our   eyes have got a "tank-ful,"   and

here we__ sit, just   cry   -   ing.   And here   we__ sit, just

Grandpa   Grandma

cry   -   ing.   Did you hear me cry?   Yes, I   heard   you cry!

Both

And   we   both know why   we're   cry   -   ing.

8 ♩

COME TO VBS

Written by David and Candy Faust
Arranged by Penny Faust

come to V - B — S!
It's that time of the year,___ The
come to V - B — S! (Oh, yes, oh, yes, it's V - B — S!)

sum-mer is here,___ The pub - lic schools are ___
Je - sus our King. ___ We learn a - bout God's ___

out.
We want some-thing to do ___ that's ___
Son.
We make so man - y crafts, ___ we have

74

spec - ial and new. ___ We need it now, there is no
lots ___ of laughs. It's so much fun for ev - 'ry

doubt.
one.

Ooh ___
(Second time only)

lots ___ of fun, Where we'll sing and we'll laugh, ___ and we'll
wan - na be cool? ___ The place you should be ___ is va -

see ev-'ry one?___   ca-tion Bi-ble school!

Come and see me, Don't say may-be, Come to V-B-

S!   Come to V-B-S!   Yes!

DISCOVERY

Written by David and Candy Faust
Arranged by Penny Faust

Bernadette sings

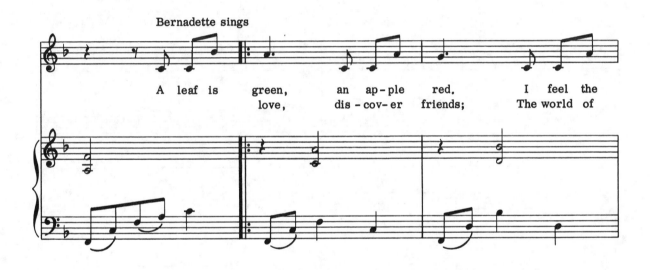

A leaf is green, an ap-ple red. I feel the
love, dis-cov-er friends; The world of

rain - drops on my head. A snow-flake white, the wa-ter
learn - ing nev-er ends. Dis-cov-er joy, dis-cov-er

blue, A star-ry night, the morn-ing dew. Our God has
song; And thank the Lord your whole life long. For God has

giv - en us so much to see and hear, to taste and touch. And as we

1.
rit. a tempo
learn, and as we grow, there is so much for us to know. Dis-cov-er
rit. a tempo

2.
rit.
learn and as we grow, there is so much for us to
rit.

78

I'M SO ANGRY

Written by David and Candy Faust
Arranged by Penny Faust

Stella

I'm so an-gry!__ I'm so mad!_____ This is the worst day _____ I've ev - er had! I should have known it was a warn-ing when I burned the toast this morn - ing, and I stubbed my toe when I got out of

bed. I'm so an-gry! I'm so peeved! And things are

worse than you'd be-lieve. So I'll yell at the dog and fuss at the cat, and

step on my lit-tle broth-er's hat, and I'll slam the door quite loud-ly when I

leave!

Spoken   Stella   Harold   Stella

I'm so mad. But Stel-la! It's not my

81

stead of blam - ing ev-'ry-one else, Why don't you hum - bly look at your - self? And

see if there's some truth in what I've said. I know you're

an- gry_____ I know you're tired. But some in - sight is re -

quired. Don't blame ev -'ry-one else for things you've done. By

pass-ing the buck, you ru-in the fun. But I've prob-a-bly said much more than you de-

Spoken

sired.   **Stella**   *hopefully* **Harold**

I   hate to ad-mit it.   Yes,

Stella   **Harold**   **Stella**

Stel-la? But you're right!   *Real-ly*, Stel-la?   You've point-ed out,   you see,

thoughtfully **Harold**   **Stella**

my re-spon-si-bil-i-ty.   Oh,   yeah.   I   need to for-give the

Stella sings

faults of oth-ers as God has for-giv-en me. I'm not so

an - gry____ an - y more. And I'm

Harold sings

She's not so an - gry____ an - y more.

sor - ry____ I've been a bore.

And she's sor - ry she's been a bore. Oth - ers'

, Both sing

But it's hard-er to see the faults in me. But we're

faults are al-ways eas-y to see,

rit.

go-ing to do much bet - ter, you will see.   Yes, we're

rit.

go-ing to do much bet-ter, you will   see!

see!   You will see,   you will   see.

JESUS AND ME

Written by David and Candy Faust
Arranged by Penny Faust

Introduction

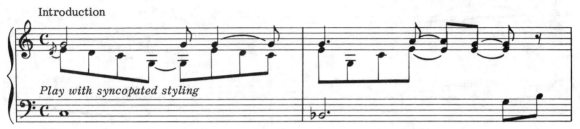

Play with syncopated styling

Harold sings

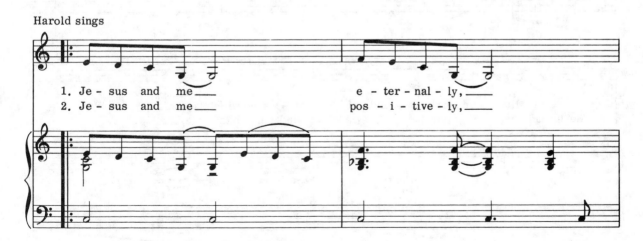

1. Je - sus and me ___ e - ter - nal - ly, ___
2. Je - sus and me ___ pos - i - tive - ly, ___

He is my Lord, ___ and He al - ways will be. ___
Life's in my fu - ture, and it al - ways will be. ___

I'm bound ___ to the one from Gal - i - lee.
I've frowned, but He brings a smile to ___ me.

Je - sus and me ___ sub - mis - sive - ly, ___
Je - sus and me ___ so lov - ing - ly, ___

I am His ser - vant, and I al - ways will be. ___
He brought sal - va - tion to a sin - ner like me. ___

I've found__ serv-ing Him is lib-er - ty.
I'm grounded on His Word so sol-id - ly.

Chorus

He__ is why_____ I am

hap-py.__ Why I am hap - py__ He is

why_____ I am__ free.__ Why I am free_____

Sock puppets sing

Sock puppets sing

He — is why———— I have so much— to live for.— He is my King,— and I will sing of Je sus and me.—

90

Je - sus and me ____ e - ter - nal - ly, ____

He is my Lord, ____ and He al - ways will be. ____

Je - sus, ____ Je - sus, ____

Je - sus and me! ____

I LOVE MY SUNDAY SCHOOL

Written by David and Candy Faust
Arranged by Penny Faust

My name is Ken-ny, and I'm

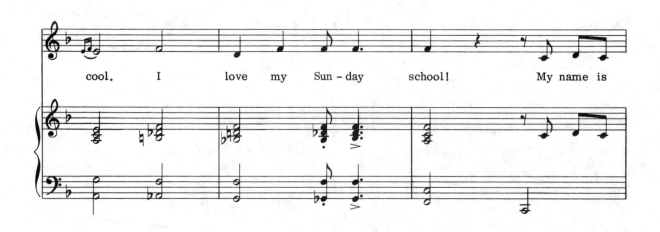

cool. I love my Sun-day school! My name is

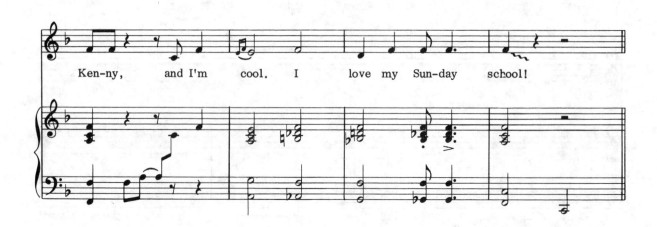

Ken-ny, and I'm cool. I love my Sun-day school!

Spoken

Hey, all you out there in audience land... I just bet you're all thinkin': "What's this dude talkin' about, anyway? I mean, what's so great about Sunday school?"

Well, if you'll tune in your ears, I'll tell you all why I think Sunday school is cool, man, real cool!

Sings

Well it's a place I go each Sun-day, and I see all of my friends. It's a

place where I can learn, and the learn-in' nev-er ends. I

learn a-bout Je-sus. My teach-er's real-ly cool. And the

Bi-ble is the Book we use; It's the great-est learn-ing tool! My name is

Ken-ny, and I'm cool. I love my Sun-day school! My name is

Ken-ny, and I'm cool. I love my Sun-day school! (Yeah!)

8

I AM THANKFUL

Written by David and Candy Faust
Arranged by Penny Faust

I am thank-ful for my God a-bove, I'm
(We are)   (our)   (we're)

thank-ful for His match-less love, I'm thank-ful for

Barney alone in last verse

to Coda

all He's done for me.

Joy to share with friends, a hope that nev-er ends, en-

96

cour - age - ment   when I'm   down;   The

prom - is - es of God,   those   words   that ring   so

true; _____

Bles - sings   like these   are ac - cep - ted   with ease,   but there's

SEE HIS GLORY

Written by David and Candy Faust
Arranged by Penny Faust

Reggae style

The Lord God reigns, let the earth be glad;___ let all the peo-ple see His glo-ry.___ The heav-ens pro-claim___ His righ-teous-ness;___ let all the peo-ple see His glo-ry.___ He cre-

(Leader)

glo - ry.___ The

Lord God reigns, let the earth be glad;___ let

all the peo - ple see His glo - ry.___ The heav - ens pro - claim___ His

righ - teous - ness;___ let all the peo - ple see His

rit.

glo - ry.___ Let all the peo - ple see His glo - ry.

HOW TO MAKE PUPPETS AND PUPPET STAGES

INSTRUCTIONS FOR MAKING PUPPETS

Harold, Stella, and the rest of the puppets are made from the inexpensive materials listed below. By following these simple instructions, you can make durable, long-lasting, attractive puppets that exhibit your own personal flair.

Materials Needed for One Puppet
- One 7" by 10" oval cut from heavy cardboard. You may be able to find oval cardboard plates this size. If not, trace a saucer or use a compass to make the two ends of your cardboard exactly the same shape.
- Foam rubber (1 to 1-1/2" thick; can usually be purchased in large squares)
- Masking tape (about two rolls)
- Red felt
- One pair men's socks
- Movable plastic eyes
- Yarn
- One baby shirt (12-month size)
- Large needle and heavy thread

Step-by-Step Instructions:
Step 1. Cut the cardboard oval in half. (Cut the rim off the paper plate.) These two pieces will form the upper and lower parts of the mouth. Try cutting a sharper curve for Hobart the Worm and Clyde the Dog. You'll end up with a more narrow head that comes to a rounded point in front.

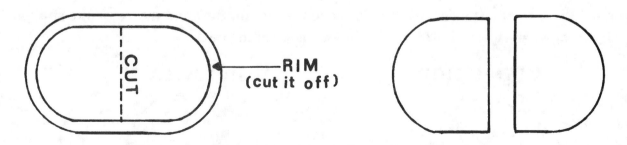

Step 2. Cut a piece of foam rubber to fit exactly onto one of the cardboard halves. Use masking tape to tape the cardboard and the foam together, leaving the straight edge open. (You will place your thumb in this opening when the puppet is finished.) Cover the cardboard and foam with tape until the whole thing is hard enough to knock on.

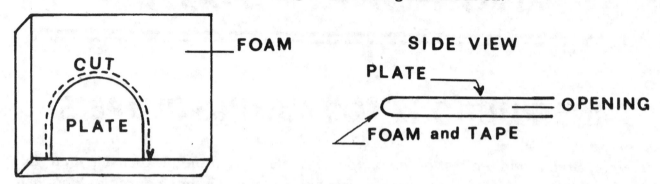

Now take the other half of the cardboard and cut another piece of foam rubber, this time making it 1-1/2 to 2" larger than the plate. (The larger the foam the higher the puppet's head will be.) Round the foam rubber over the cardboard. The edge of the foam will fit flat on the cardboard and the excess will rise up in the middle. This is where your four fingers will fit in the puppet's head. Tape the foam onto the cardboard, thoroughly covering both with tape (but, of course, leaving the back open).

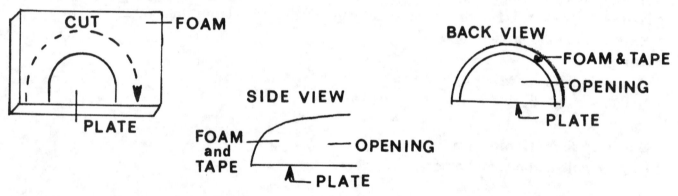

This top portion of the puppet's head will be a little more difficult to make than the bottom was, but it will turn out all right. Keep the foam rounded as you tape it, and keep taping until you can knock on the puppet's head (don't be afraid to use a lot of tape; the head needs to be *hard*).

Step 3. Place the two pieces together to make the mouth. Sew and then tape the straight edges together. Again, don't tape up the openings in the back.

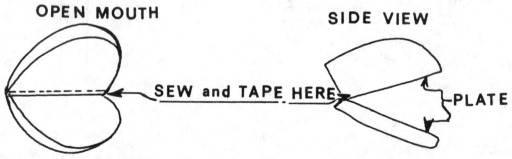

Step 4. Take one of the socks and pull it over the top part of the head from front to back. This will be difficult to do, but it is possible. Make sure that enough of the sock is left hanging over the back of the head that it will reach down to the puppet's body. The other half of the sock will bunch up inside the puppet's mouth and will have to be cut off so that the mouth can close. The toe will not fit over the head, so cut it off. Stretch the other sock over the bottom jaw of the puppet, making sure that the top of the sock hangs down off the back of the jaw. Again, cut off the toe of the sock and the part that is bunched up inside the mouth.

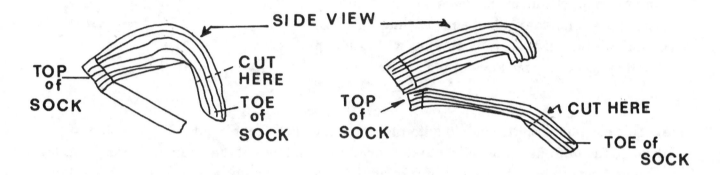

After you have cut off the excess parts of the socks, fold each sock tightly and sew it neatly onto the inside of the mouth—the top sock onto the "roof" of the mouth, and the bottom sock onto the bottom. The inside of the mouth can get too bulky, so cut off as much of the sock as possible to allow the mouth to open and close freely.

An alternative method to steps three and four is to draw the socks over the top and bottom parts of the head before you join them together. You will still have to cut off parts of the socks in order to join the straight edges of the back of the head, but this method may leave you with fewer wrinkles and bunched-up sock inside the mouth.

Cut a piece of felt into the exact shape of the mouth and sew it onto the inside of the mouth (glue does not work). The felt will cover up the sewn part of the sock.

Now sew what is left of the socks hanging off the back into a tube that will reach down into the puppet's clothes. Your hand and part of your arm will fit through this tube.

Step 5. Using yarn, create the hairstyle you want (braids, curls, etc.) Cut a big bunch of yarn into strands of equal length. Sew these strands into a mat on a sewing machine and then hand-sew onto the puppet's head. Trim and arrange into a hairstyle. Curls can be made by dipping short pieces of yarn into fabric stiffener, arranging them on waxed paper and allowing them to dry. Then sew the curls onto the puppet's head. Sew a mat of yarn on a sewing machine, fold in half and sew into place for Grandpa's beard. Make the hair mats wide enough that they will cover the back of the puppet's head.

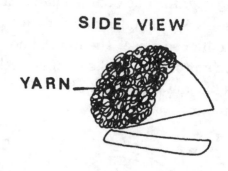

SIDE VIEW

YARN

Step 6. Sew a baby shirt securely onto the top of the sock. Your hand and arm will pass through the bottom of the shirt into the sock, into the head of the puppet. If your hand flops around inside the head of the puppet, stuff the head with foam rubber until your hand fits securely.

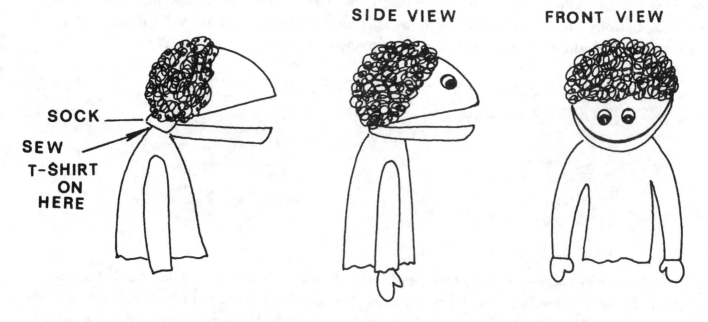

SIDE VIEW   FRONT VIEW

SOCK

SEW
T-SHIRT
ON
HERE

Step 7. Stuff the arms of the shirt with foam rubber and use the toes of the socks to make little hands for the puppet. Sew the hands onto the arms of the shirt. Now glue the eyes on, and your puppet is nearing completion. Use your imagination and add whatever else you would like your puppet to have: a nose, freckles, teeth, a body, movable arms, a funny hat, glasses, a mustache or beard, etc. Personalize your puppet! Be creative!

ADAPTING THESE INSTRUCTIONS
TO MAKE ANIMAL PUPPETS

Dog and Worm:

Follow basic directions through Step 2. Then take one of the socks and pull it up over the top part of the head (the rounded part). Do *not* cut off the toe. Instead, pull the whole sock (including the toe) completely over the head. The whole top of the sock should be left hanging from the back of the head. Do the same for the bottom jaw.

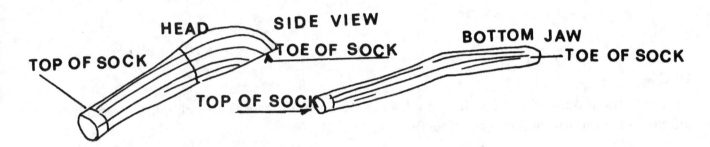

Cut off about one-fourth of each sock lengthwise, then proceed with Step 3.

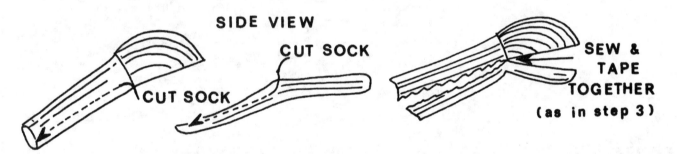

Sew the socks together on the inside of the mouth. Then sew the sides of the socks together to make one large sock.

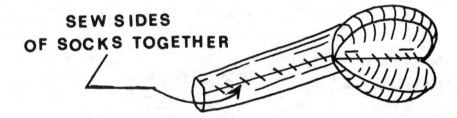

107

Dog:

   Make ears by cutting off the tops of another pair of socks and sewing the ends of them to the head. (Ears may also be made from pieces of felt.) Cut a long, floppy tongue from a piece of red felt and sew it to the inside of the mouth. Add a nose (a ball of foam rubber wrapped in cloth and sewed to the face) and two big eyes made of felt.

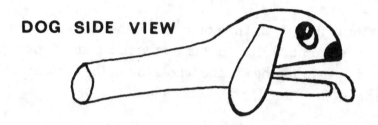

DOG SIDE VIEW

Worm:

   Cover the mouth with felt as in Step 4. Glue on eyes. If desired, use chenille wire to make antennae for the top of the head. Sew them on.

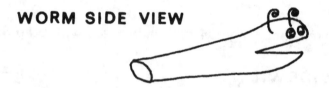

WORM SIDE VIEW

Elephant:

   Instead of making a flat lower jaw (as in Step 2), make two of the large, rounded portions of the head and use one of them for the lower jaw.

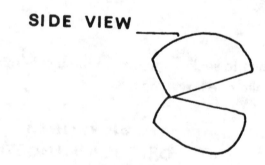

SIDE VIEW

   To make the trunk: before pulling the sock over the top part of the head, stuff about 8 inches of it with foam rubber or a cardboard tube. (The tube from a paper towel roll works well.)

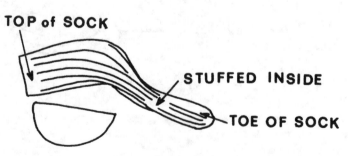

TOP of SOCK

STUFFED INSIDE

TOE OF SOCK

Make ears out of cardboard, cover with socks that match the color of the rest of the head, and sew to the head. (A loose flexible sock made of terry cloth or something similar works best for the elephant.) Note: You will need *two* pairs of socks to make the elephant (one pair for the head and jaw, and one pair for the ears).

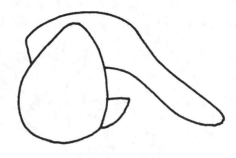

Make the elephant's body with a T-shirt in Step 6) or with a square of foam rubber taped into a tube shape and covered with fabric.

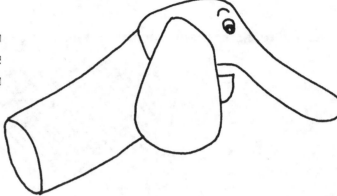

Alligator:

The alligator is made the same was as the basic puppet with one variation. Follow Steps 1 and 2. Then cut another plate (or oval) in the same way as in Step 1.

Take both halves of the second paper plate and cut out foam rubber to fit exactly flat onto the plate halves. Tape the plate halves and the foam together using masking tape.

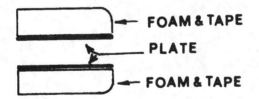

Securely tape the second plate halves to the first plate halves.

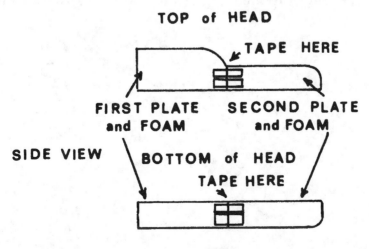

109

When following Steps 3 and 4 you will be working with a longer head. You will need to use long socks to cover this puppet. After you cover the head with a sock, it should look like this:

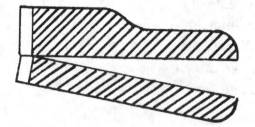

Make eyes and teeth for the puppet using felt or any other materials available.

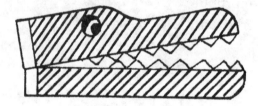

Optional: You can make a body for the alligator using the instructions for the elephant's body.

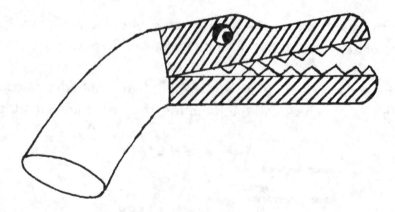

To make a sock puppet, take a sock and glue or sew two eyes on it. Add yarn for hair if you like. Put your hand in the sock and work the mouth with your hand. That's all there is to it!

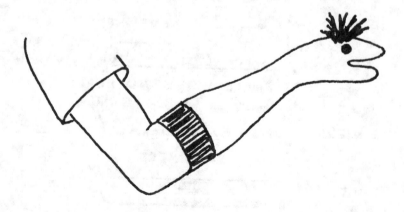

INSTRUCTIONS FOR MAKING A PUPPET STAGE

Materials Needed:

- 1-1/2" plastic water pipe (usually can be purchased in 10-foot lengths). Cut to the dimensions shown below.

- Plastic fittings: two 90° elbow joints, two "T" fittings, one arm of the T having a 45° angle (or some combination of fittings that will produce the structure shown below).

- Four thick, wooden bases (the heavier the better) with a 1-1/2" hole drilled in each one to give support to the stage so it won't tip over.

- Curtain made from 16 to 18 yards of dark material heavy enough that you can't see through it.

- Optional: Microphone stands with heavy metal bases can be used to support the stage. Just slip the upright pipes over the mike stands. (If you use these, you will not need the wooden bases.)

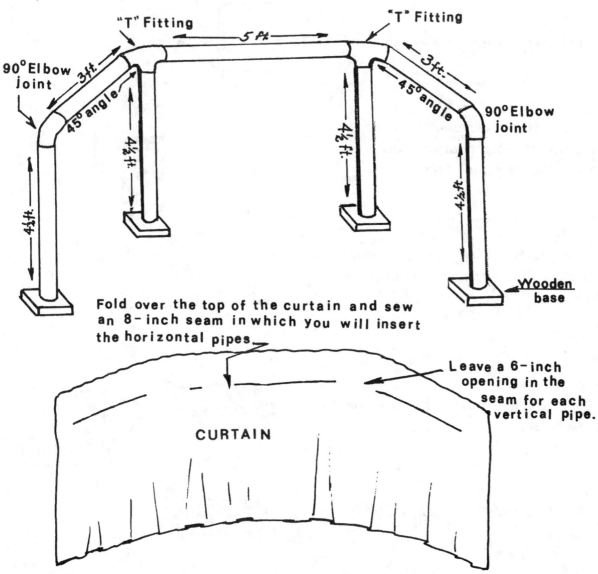

111

The stage made from plastic pipe has many advantages. It is lightweight yet sturdy; it is relatively inexpensive; it is easy to transport (its various sections are small enough to fit in the trunk of most cars).

If you are prohibited, however, by space, time, or financial limitations from building and using this stage, perhaps one of the following ideas will serve to meet your needs; or, if you need an "instant stage," try one of these:

- A large, collapsible cardboard partition

- A piano. (You might even want the puppet to converse with the pianist!)

- A folding table turned on its side.

- A tension rod or expandable clothes rod extended across a doorway, with a small curtain hanging from the rod.

- A window. (Have the puppets appear in the window while the children sit outdoors on the grass.)

- A blanket hanging over a line fastened to poles or trees.

- As a last resort, a blanket held by two people.

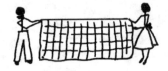